STUDENT UNIT GUIDE

AQA | A2 | UNIT 4A

Government & Politics

The Government of the USA

Colleen Harris

Series Editor: Eric Magee

Philip Allan Updates, an imprint of Hodder Education, an Hachette UK company, Market Place, Deddington, Oxfordshire OX15 0SE

Orders

Bookpoint Ltd, 130 Milton Park, Abingdon, Oxfordshire OX14 4SB
tel: 01235 827827
fax: 01235 400401
e-mail: education@bookpoint.co.uk
Lines are open 9.00 a.m.–5.00 p.m., Monday to Saturday, with a 24-hour message answering service. You can also order through the Philip Allan Updates website: www.philipallan.co.uk

© Philip Allan Updates 2009

ISBN 978-0-340-98708-7

First printed 2009
Impression number 5 4 3
Year 2014 2013 2012 2011

This guide has been written specifically to support students preparing for the AQA A2 Government & Politics Unit 4A examination. The content has been neither approved nor endorsed by AQA and remains the sole responsibility of the author.

Typeset by Phoenix Photosetting, Chatham, Kent
Printed by MPG Books, Bodmin

Hachette UK's policy is to use papers that are natural, renewable and recyclable products and made from wood grown in sustainable forests. The logging and manufacturing processes are expected to conform to the environmental regulations of the country of origin.

Contents

Introduction

How to use this guide 4

The specification explained 4

The unit test explained 6

Assessment objectives at A2 7

Levels of response 7

How to do well in Unit 4A 8

Preparation for examination day 10

Examination day 10

How to achieve top grades 12

■ ■ ■

Content Guidance

About this section 14

The constitutional framework of US government 15

The legislative branch of government: US Congress 27

The executive branch of government 41

The judicial branch of government: the Supreme Court 53

■ ■ ■

Questions and Answers

About this section 66

Question 1 The constitutional framework of US government 67

Question 2 The legislative branch of government: US Congress 72

Question 3 The executive branch of government 78

Question 4 The judicial branch of government: the Supreme Court 83

Introduction

This guide has been written to help students opting for AQA Unit 4A, The Government of the USA, to prepare more effectively. Its aim is to provide students with a clear outline of the way in which the unit is structured and examined, as well as a summary of the content for each part of the unit. Unit 3A, The Politics of the USA, is covered in a separate unit guide.

How to use this guide

This guide is divided into three sections:
- The **Introduction** outlines the main aims of the guide, a general overview of the unit, information on assessment, the skills needed for success, more general advice on approaching A2 study, and revision and examination advice.
- The **Content Guidance** section looks at the core content of the unit, focusing on the four areas covered in the specification, including key concepts and theories. The greater focus at A2 on analysis and evaluation is stressed, as well as the need for the effective use of evidence and examples to back up arguments.
- The **Questions and Answers** section includes candidate responses to examination questions at A2, explaining why candidates gain, or fail to gain, higher-level marks for their responses and how examination responses could be improved to achieve higher marks and grades.

The specification explained

The specification for this unit is divided into four broad areas of study:
- The constitutional framework of US government: the significance of the codified Constitution to the workings of US government and its underlying principles, including the separation of powers, checks and balances, federalism and entrenched rights; the nature of constitutional change and the importance of the Constitution to US government today.
- The legislative branch of government: the main role, powers and functions of the bicameral Congress and its relationship to the other branches of government; the party and committee systems within it and its social composition.
- The executive branch of government: the formal and informal powers of the president and the relationship between the executive and the other branches of government, including the constraints on the exercise of power; the roles and functions of other parts of the executive branch, such as the cabinet, the Executive Office of the President and the federal bureaucracy.
- The judicial branch of government: the role of the Supreme Court in constitutional interpretation and judicial review, its relationship with the other branches of government, the way it is appointed and debates about its political role and power and the impact of its judgements.

introduction

Although not specifically required, it will be beneficial at the beginning of your course on American government for you to have some basic knowledge of US history and some of the most important events and presidencies that have shaped the way government works. This will promote contextual awareness and so aid your general understanding of the unit.

Specification at a glance

The AQA Unit 4A specification below shows in more detail the key concepts associated with each of the four parts of the unit. It also provides helpful amplification of the core content of the unit as a guide for studying, revision and exam practice.

The constitutional framework of US government

Key concepts	Content and amplification
• Fundamental law • Codified constitution • Limited government • Flexibility/rigidity • Federalism • Decentralisation and states' rights • Constitutional sovereignty • Entrenched rights • Constitutional interpretation	• The nature and significance of the US Constitution and the framework of government that it lays down • The importance of the constitutional principles of the separation of powers and checks and balances to the operation of government and the way that these apply in practice today • The significance of the Bill of Rights • The amendment process • The federal system of government and its implications • The relationship between the federal government and the states • Constitutional change and its causes and effects • Debates concerning the importance of the US Constitution to the working of US government today • The Supreme Court and the Constitution • Comparisons with the UK's uncodified constitution and unitary system to illustrate arguments

The legislative branch of government: US Congress

Key concepts	Content and amplification
• Bicameralism • Gridlock • Presidential veto and congressional override • Impeachment • Advice and consent powers • Pork-barrelling • Filibuster	• The constitutional role and power(s) of the US Congress • The composition of Congress and the different terms of office • The differences between the House and the Senate and the relationship between the two houses • Debates concerning the functions, powers and effectiveness of Congress in legislation, oversight and the power of the purse • The importance of both the party system and the committee system within Congress • The representative role of Senators and Representatives • Debates concerning the social composition of Congress • The relationship of Congress with the executive branch and the Supreme Court • Comparisons with the Westminster Parliament to illustrate arguments

The executive branch of government

Key concepts	Content and amplification
• Presidential executive • Imperial presidency • Imperilled presidency • Veto • Power to persuade • Bureaucratic power • Iron triangles • Spoils system • Clientelism	• The Constitution and the executive branch of government • Debates concerning presidential power, both formal and informal, and the ability to actually exercise it in both domestic and foreign policy • Limitations and constraints on executive power from the Constitution, Congress and the Supreme Court • Debates concerning the main determinants of presidential–congressional relations. The ebb and flow of power • The nature of the exercise of power within the executive branch • Debates concerning the relative power and influence of the cabinet and the Executive Office of the President • The role of the federal bureaucracy and the federal agencies • Comparisons with the UK executive to illustrate arguments

The judicial branch of government: the Supreme Court

Key concepts	Content and amplification
• Constitutional interpretation • Judicial review • Original intent • Judicial activism and restraint • Strict and loose constructionism • Judicial power • Entrenched rights	• The constitutional role of the Supreme Court and the nature of judicial power • The Supreme Court's role as guardian of the Constitution through constitutional interpretation • The Supreme Court's power of judicial review since 1803 • Debates and controversies surrounding the selection and appointment process of Supreme Court justices • The political significance of the Supreme Court and the impact of its landmark judgements • The protection of citizens' rights by the Supreme Court • The relationship of the Supreme Court with the other branches of government • Comparison with the senior judiciary in the UK to illustrate arguments

The unit test explained

Unit 4A is 90 minutes in length and you must answer two questions from a choice of four. The questions will reflect the four parts of the unit shown above. All the specification topics will be covered and it would be unwise not to cover all topics in your revision.

Each of the four questions has two parts:
- Part (a) is worth 10 marks and is a short-answer question. This should be completed in around 8–10 minutes. If you spend more time on this you will eat into the time needed to complete the more mark-rich and challenging essays.

- Part (b) is worth 30 marks and is an extended essay. At least 30–35 minutes should be spent on each of the two essays chosen.

The two parts will be connected in the sense that they are part of the same topic area being assessed. They are not necessarily connected in any other way, to prevent any possible overlap in the answers given to both questions.

Assessment objectives at A2

Although the three assessment objectives at A2 are the same as at AS, they are weighted differently. At A2 more marks are awarded for analysis (AO2) than for knowledge (AO1).

AO1: Demonstrate *knowledge* and *understanding* of relevant institutions, processes, political concepts, theories and debates. AS weighting 50%; A2 weighting 45%.

AO2: *Analyse* and *evaluate* political information, arguments and explanations, and identify parallels, connections, similarities and differences between aspects of the political systems studied. AS weighting 30%; A2 weighting 35%.

AO3: *Construct* and *communicate* coherent arguments, making use of a range of appropriate political vocabulary. Here the weighting of 20% is the same at AS and A2.

When you write your answer both to part (a) and part (b), you will be given marks for all three of these assessment objectives. These will be totalled to give the mark for each part of the question, with a maximum score of 40 (10 + 30) for each question. The total mark for the unit is 80. This means that the total mark can be achieved in a variety of ways, and students may show different strengths or weaknesses in their answers. Generally, a very good student will achieve high marks on all three assessment objectives, as the answer will demonstrate high levels of knowledge and understanding and excellent analytical skills, will have structure and coherence, and will contain impressive political vocabulary. However, it is possible to gain high marks for one objective and lower marks for another. For example, a student's knowledge of a topic may be impressive but the answer may lack clear focus and analysis and it may not be clearly communicated. This means the mark may be high on AO1 but lower on AO2 and AO3. You should be aware of these assessment objectives and practise them throughout the year in homework essays, timed essays in class and research assignments that develop your independent research skills.

Levels of response

A2 assessment uses a generic mark scheme including levels of response, which examiners follow in order to allocate marks to students' answers. There is also a mark scheme for each specific question, reflecting the content expected in the answer.

Level 4 is the highest level of response. Students who achieve marks at the top of this level will have written answers which are comprehensive, fully address the requirements of the question, give clear and accurate evidence and excellent examples, and include developed theories and concepts, communicating clearly and effectively with focus, direction and conclusions. These are high A students.

Level 3 responses are 'good' rather than 'excellent'. Students 'clearly' rather than 'comprehensively' address the requirements of the question and give 'good' evidence and examples, communicated 'well'.

Level 2 responses are characterised by the key word 'limited'. At this level of response, students show limited knowledge, with a limited attempt to address the requirements of the question, limited evidence, examples and concepts, and communication which is limited in clarity, vocabulary, focus and direction.

Level 1 responses should be avoided at all costs. At the bottom of this level it is barely worth entering the examination room. The key word here is 'little': the student shows little in terms of knowledge, focus, evidence, examples and clear communication. These responses are usually simplistic or superficial narrative with little sign of serious study.

How to do well in Unit 4A

It is important to recognise that A2 units are more demanding than AS units. After a year of studying AS Government and Politics, however, the groundwork has been covered, so that the greater A2 challenges can be faced with confidence. Believe your teachers when they tell you that the work will become harder, and rise to the challenge!

Make sure that you are very familiar with the Unit 4A specification, including:
- the four areas of the unit content on which questions will be based
- the number of questions on the paper and the marks for each section
- the choice of questions and the type of questions
- the assessment objectives and the levels of response

You can get a copy of the AQA specification through the website **www.aqa.org.uk**. This includes sample questions, mark schemes and the generic assessment criteria discussed above, which should guide your studies.

Read

From day one, be prepared to read widely around the subject to broaden and deepen your knowledge of American government. This should include:
- UK and US quality newspapers and websites and their coverage of American government, such as Supreme Court cases, the actions of the president or events

in Congress. Using these resources can be particularly rewarding in terms of picking up contemporary evidence and examples and also in reinforcing and extending a general interest in the subject matter of the unit.

- up-to-date textbooks on American government and politics
- articles in *Politics Review* that are focused on specific topics, which can then be used to reinforce your class notes
- current affairs journals such as *Time* or *Newsweek* and *The Economist* (which includes an excellent American Survey section) which have extensive coverage of American issues that should stimulate as well as inform
- A. J. Bennett's *US Government and Politics Annual Survey*, published by Philip Allan Updates

Watch

Watch the television news regularly, paying special attention to information about American government, to update your notes.

Note

Use notebooks to record significant developments or events in American government, such as a controversial Senate filibuster or a proposed constitutional amendment, otherwise some key changes and events that take place while you are studying will be forgotten. These notes can be a very effective supplement to your textbook and class notes.

File

Try to keep an organised file from the beginning of your course, filing your notes in an order that makes sense to you and can be understood by you. Keep notes in see-through wallets and label and index them carefully. It is then possible to summarise these notes on index cards during your intensive revision programme at the end.

Review

Much advice to students concentrates on a revision programme at the end of the course, and such a programme is certainly essential. However, it is probably more important to review your notes on a regular basis — this means you are learning as you go along, avoiding last-minute panics. Revision means revisiting, but this should be revisiting specification topics that you *already know*, not trying to learn them from scratch for the examinations. Pay particular attention throughout the course to topics that you have found especially difficult or uninteresting, and that you do not feel you have quite grasped. Do not wait until the revision period to try to work them out. They are as likely to appear on the examination paper as the topics that you have found easier or more interesting. Last-minute panic revision of topics not fully under-stood should always be avoided, as it is rarely successful.

Preparation for examination day

The period of revising your notes before the examination is crucial and should be taken very seriously. Here are some useful tips:

Do what works best for you

This may seem a strange piece of advice, but students do revise in different ways, using different methods and with variable results. You may prefer to revise late at night or early in the morning, in silence or with music, alone or with friends, in long stretches or in short bursts with treats built in. Just do whatever works for you.

Reduce your notes to manageable proportions

It helps to rewrite or reformat your notes, using headings, bullet points, lists or spider diagrams, and different colours for emphasis or effect. Once you have done this, you can transfer all the key points that need to be known onto revision index cards, with one card for each part of a topic. This will make learning much more manageable. You might also put different coloured sticky notes or aide-memoires all over your room, with key terms or facts that you need to remember. Interesting and helpful quotes that you have discovered can also be learnt in this way.

Revise all four areas of the unit

Remember, there are no predictable questions, and if you revise selectively, leaving large gaps in your revision programme, it could be disastrous for your result. Revise all four areas of the unit as laid out in the specification. Don't bank on certain questions coming up, and don't prepare for specific questions that you hope will be on the paper or the ones that were there last year. The A or B grade that you were expecting could easily turn into a C or D, and it is too late for regrets when you leave the exam room.

Focus on weak areas

When revising, concentrate particularly on your known areas of weakness and areas that you actively dislike. This will be your last chance to sort out these difficult areas before you possibly encounter them when you turn over the examination paper on the day. The inward groan that arises is not a pleasant feeling!

Examination day

There's an old saying: 'Those who fail to prepare are preparing to fail.' If you really have prepared, the examination gives you the chance to show what you know and can do. On examination day, however, there are certain pitfalls that you must avoid if you are to fulfil your potential and achieve the grade you deserve.

- Arrive at the right time on the right day, with the right equipment (black pens) and the right attitude. Avoid last-minute panic revision or chatter with friends about how little you know or how you are going to fail. Be positive.
- When you turn over the exam paper, spend time making the right choice concerning which two questions out of the four to answer. Look at all four very carefully before making your choice. Many students realise halfway through answering a question that they have made the wrong choice, but by then it is too late to go back. A few minutes spent at the start making the wisest choice will not be wasted.
- When you have identified the two questions that you think will allow you to gain the highest marks, think carefully about planning your answer. Do not begin to write until you have collected your thoughts and made a brief plan (not a collection of random thoughts) about the direction in which you wish your answer to go. This applies particularly to essay questions that need a coherent structure in order to gain high marks. As you are writing, other ideas may come to you that you had not thought of originally. Jot them down within your plan so that you can incorporate them into your essay later. Too often it is only when students leave the room at the end of the exam that they remember the crucial arguments they have omitted.
- Get your timing right. You should answer the (a) questions on Unit 4A in approximately 8–10 minutes, leaving enough time to write a full answer to the (b) essay questions and to check your work at the end.
- The key word for examination success is *focus*. The reason why many students do not do as well as expected, or do not achieve the grade they were hoping for, is that they fail to answer the question that has been asked. A good answer plan should help you to avoid straying from the question and drifting into answering another question that has not been asked.
- Exam questions never ask you to 'write all you know' or simply to 'describe'. There are key 'command' words, such as 'explain' or 'evaluate', and you should follow them. Many students do worse than they or their teachers expect because they do not do this. If a question asks, 'How far do you agree' or 'To what extent', this means that some debate is implied within the question and you should address this debate in your response.
- Always make sure that you have at least one piece of supporting evidence or an example to back up the argument you are making. Far too many students make sweeping assertions, or do not develop their arguments with evidence and examples, and this reduces the potential mark available. At A2 try to introduce some kind of supporting theory into your answer, for example theories of judicial activism and restraint when discussing the Supreme Court. Try to achieve a balance between knowledge, theory, analysis, supporting evidence and examples.
- Contextual awareness is part of a good student response. All political events and processes take place within a context, and your answer should reflect this. Pages of historical introduction are not necessary, but there is little doubt that knowing, for example, how and why the Supreme Court 'discovered' its power of judicial

review or how the presidency or federalism has developed and changed helps to provide the context in which understanding of American government takes place.

How to achieve top grades

- Make sure you have covered all the specification topics in your revision.
- Consult mark schemes and assessment objectives to understand how examiners will mark your answers.
- Answer the question that has been set, not the one you wish had been set.
- Analyse the question. Identify key words in the question and refer to them in your answer where possible.
- Keep a tight focus on the question asked, in the introduction, in the middle and at the end. Don't drift.
- Use examples and evidence to back up your arguments at all times.
- Show contextual awareness and understanding wherever possible.
- Use political concepts, theories and vocabulary, quoting political scientists such as Neustadt or political thinkers such as Montesquieu if possible.
- Avoid model answers based on questions set in previous papers, especially when the wording of a question has changed and a different response is required.
- Use your time well: don't repeat points, and don't conclude your answer by simply repeating all you have said before.
- Avoid simplistic assertions and sweeping generalisations in your answers. Do not give your personal opinions or use the word 'I'.
- Be aware of debates surrounding topics. The answer to many questions to do with government is, 'It depends', and valid arguments can be identified on both sides.
- Make sure you use a good writing style. Write with clarity and direction, with good grammar, vocabulary, spelling and legibility, to make a good overall impression on the examiner, who is going to give you a mark for your communication skills. Essays that gain high marks will have a good introduction setting the essay in context, well developed and convincing arguments, and a conclusion that draws the threads together.
- Students who enter the examination room unprepared and lacking in serious study, and whose answers are unfocused, confused and poorly written, with little evidence of knowledge, understanding and analytical and communication skills, are unlikely to achieve the grade they wish for — but may get the grade they deserve.

Content
Guidance

This section of the guide aims to address the key areas of content of the four sections of the AQA Unit 4A specification: the constitutional framework of US government; the legislative branch of government: US Congress; the executive branch of government; and the judicial branch of government: the Supreme Court. It focuses on the main theories, issues and debates in these four areas and contains the key concepts that you need to know and understand. Reference is also made to comparative features with the UK system of government, to facilitate the synoptic understanding required at A2. While making no claim to cover every possible aspect of the four specification areas in detail, the content guidance aims to provide concise but thorough coverage of the core topics. This material is best used as the basis for further study and research; you are encouraged to find additional examples and evidence from other sources, including those from contemporary developments in the ever-changing government of the USA.

The constitutional framework of US government

The starting point for the study of the government of the United States of America is the US Constitution. The original document, written in Philadelphia in 1787 by the Founding Fathers, in seven articles of over 7,000 words, is the oldest written constitution. A product of the revolutionary war of independence and struggle against the tyranny of colonial rule, its provisions were influenced by the writings of political theorists such as Locke and Montesquieu. It represented a sharp turn in US history and the beginning of the world's first modern democracy.

The US Constitution is as important to the understanding of the operation of US government today as it was in the eighteenth century.

What is a constitution and what do constitutions do?

A constitution is an authoritative set of rules that seeks to establish the role, powers and functions of the institutions of government (legislative, executive and judicial), regulate the relationships between them and define the relationship between the state and its citizens. A constitution can be both written and unwritten, and codified or uncodified.

Why is the American Constitution so important?

- It is the supreme law of the USA. Constitutional law is fundamental or higher law, providing the rules that govern the government.
- It is the source of, but also a limitation on, the power of government.
- It provides for governments to have enough power to be strong and effective, while at the same time protecting the individual liberties of citizens against the abuse of that power.
- It balances the need for a strong federal government with the need to give autonomy to the states.
- It is codified in a single document and entrenched.

Key principles

There were four main provisions laid down in the Constitution:
- **Representative and accountable government** through the provision of fixed-term elections held every 4 years for the president and every 2 years for the House of Representatives. (The Senate was not directly elected until 1913.)

- The **separation of powers**, with the three branches of government (legislative, executive and judicial) separated through the first three articles of the Constitution. These powers were then subject to **checks and balances**.
- A **federal structure** of government, with power divided between the federal government in Washington and the individual states.
- There was to be **limited government**, with citizens given inalienable and entrenched rights in the Bill of Rights, added in 1791.

These were revolutionary changes at the time. With only minor amendment since, they still form the basis of the operation of US government today. They are therefore crucial to the understanding of the workings of the executive, legislature and judiciary in the USA at the different levels of government.

The separation of powers

The principle was adopted from the writings of Montesquieu in 1748. Montesquieu stressed the need to avoid tyranny by fragmenting the power of government through the device of the separation of powers (which he mistakenly believed to exist in the English system of government). The theory is that each of the functions of government (passing laws, executing laws and adjudicating on laws) should be exercised by a different branch — the legislature (Article 1, Congress), the executive (Article 2, President) and the judiciary (Article 3, Supreme Court) — in order to avoid tyranny and to protect liberty. Power would not be concentrated in one branch of government but separated between the branches.

The theory implies independence of the branches of government. It implies that there should be a separation of personnel, with no overlap between the three branches. This is why Barack Obama and Hillary Clinton, for example, had to give up their Senate seats when becoming president and secretary of state.

However, the theory also implies the interdependence of the branches of government through the associated checks and balances placed on each of them, particularly the legislative and executive branches, to prevent any one from becoming too powerful. 'Ambition will be used to counteract ambition,' said Madison. This is why American political scientist Richard Neustadt described the American system not as a 'separation of powers' (which would mean that nothing could ever work) but as 'separate institutions sharing powers', where power is very difficult to exercise but where the branches have to work together to get things done.

Checks and balances in the USA

The following are some examples of the checks and balances in the system:
- Congress has legislative power but this power is checked by the presidential veto.
- The presidential veto is checked by the use of a congressional override with a two-thirds majority in both houses of Congress.

- The Supreme Court can decide that laws (and actions) are unconstitutional through its power of judicial review, which it 'discovered' in the 1803 *Marbury* v *Madison* case.
- The president is the commander-in-chief of the armed forces but only Congress can declare (and fund) war.
- Presidential appointments need to be confirmed and presidential treaties need to be ratified with the 'advice and consent' of the Senate.

So the branches of US government can constrain each other's power.

Criticisms

It has been argued that the system offers an 'invitation to struggle', to the executive and legislative branches in particular, and can be a recipe for institutional gridlock, with little being achieved as a result of power struggles between the branches. This is particularly the case when there is divided government in Washington, with the branches controlled by different parties (encouraged by the constitutional provision of staggered elections). It is likely that this was the intention of the Founding Fathers, who wished, above all, to restrain the exercise of power and avoid its concentration in the executive branch. Many have argued that this has led to weak government, inertia and difficulty in making decisions, especially controversial ones.

An alternative argument, however, is that the system means that the branches of government *must* work cooperatively for anything to be done, and that this leads to more consensus seeking, negotiation and compromise to achieve common goals and solutions.

We return to the relationships between the branches of government in later parts of this section in the context of the US Congress, the presidency and the Supreme Court.

Constitutional change

A key debate surrounding the role of a constitution in the political life of a nation is how easily it can adapt to changing circumstances and conditions. Put simply, this relates to arguments about whether constitutions are rigid or flexible, easy or difficult to change. The reality is that *all* constitutions, whether codified or not, have some degree of both rigidity *and* flexibility.

The Founding Fathers recognised the need to safeguard constitutional rules from the 'whims' of 'temporary' governments and, although 'ordinary law' is made in Congress (subject to judicial review by the Supreme Court since 1803), the Constitution itself was deliberately made difficult to change. Nevertheless, it would not be correct to describe it as rigid; indeed it has been described as a living document, still relevant today.

How can the US Constitution be changed?

Change through the formal amendment process (Article 5)

Formal constitutional amendment is a tortuous process, requiring supermajorities of at least two-thirds of the vote in *both* houses of Congress, followed by ratification by three-quarters of the state legislatures (meaning 13 states could block any constitutional change).

This process entails a prolonged period of debate and demands a clear consensus in favour of change, thus avoiding hasty decisions made without adequate thought. As a result, there have been only 27 amendments to the Constitution since it was written. This number includes the first ten amendments, the Bill of Rights, ratified in 1791.

Most proposed amendments fail to attract the required support. Examples include:
- a balanced budget amendment — this would never pass in Congress
- an equal rights amendment — this failed to get the required states' vote
- making abortion, same-sex marriage or flag burning unconstitutional

Examples of successful constitutional amendments include:
- the civil rights amendments following the Civil War (Thirteenth, Fourteenth and Fifteenth amendments)
- direct election for the Senate (Seventeenth Amendment, 1913)
- amendments to extend voting rights — to women (Nineteenth Amendment, 1921) and to age 18 (Twenty-sixth Amendment, 1971)
- two-term presidency (Twenty-second Amendment, 1951)

The other way of getting a formal change to the Constitution is through the calling of a constitutional convention by two-thirds of the states. This method has never been used.

Change through Supreme Court interpretation

'We live under a Constitution, but the Constitution is what the judges say it is.' (Chief Justice Hughes, 1909)

The US Constitution is a short document containing some vague language. It is likely that the Founding Fathers intended it to be open to interpretation in future times and not be regarded as a tablet of stone forever set in eighteenth-century conditions. The amendments are also written in general rather than specific language: for example, the Fourteenth Amendment's 'equal protection of the laws' and the Eighth Amendment's banning of 'cruel and unusual' punishment.

The interpretation of the meaning of the words of the Constitution and its amendments is the function of the Supreme Court, through the cases brought before it. The words themselves do not change (they are simply 'words on paper'), but their meaning is subject to revision and updating through judicial interpretation. Such revisions are referred to as 'interpretative amendments' rather than formal changes.

The same phrases in the Constitution may be interpreted differently at different times and in different circumstances; for example, the phrase 'equal protection of the laws' in the Fourteenth Amendment was interpreted one way in the *Plessy v Ferguson* case of 1896, but very differently in the *Brown* v *Board of Education of Topeka* case in 1954. The growth of presidential powers from the 1930s and the shift of authority from state to federal government are similarly the result of Supreme Court interpretation of the Constitution.

The Constitution is therefore more flexible and less rigid than is commonly thought. US government has been able to evolve in response to new challenges and demands that have arisen through changing conditions and circumstances, such as civil war, great depression, foreign wars, Watergate and presidential impeachment.

Change through developing conventions

It is said that all constitutions are incomplete guides to the realities and practice of politics and government within any state. All constitutions, including the American, are a blend of both written and unwritten rules. The US Constitution refers to broad principles only and lays down a loose framework of government. As a result, many of the ways in which government in the USA today actually works in practice are not in the Constitution and have no constitutional status. Rather, they have evolved to fill in the gaps where the Constitution is silent. Examples would include:

- the existence and workings of the cabinet, the Executive Office of the President (EXOP) and the federal bureaucracy
- the huge power of the congressional committees, and the Supreme Court's power of judicial review, neither of which is constitutionally derived

When the US Constitution was written in 1787, it was for a country with 3 million inhabitants in 13 states, facing relatively simple issues that needed to be resolved. It is that same document, plus amendments, which is now providing the framework of government for a world superpower, a country of over 300 million inhabitants in 50 states, facing highly complex economic, social and foreign policy issues. The US Constitution has been described as 'brilliantly adaptive' despite its codified nature, as it has changed and evolved to meet these new conditions. It can be judged by how well it has stood the test of time.

The strengths and weaknesses of the codified American Constitution

Major strengths

- Sovereignty is with the Constitution and its major principles are entrenched, safe from interference from a temporary government.
- It constrains the exercise of power by the different branches of government, thus avoiding the development of an 'elective dictatorship'.
- Individual liberties are entrenched and widely known and supported.
- It contains the flexibility to be amended in response to changing political conditions.

- Its provisions are safeguarded by the independent Supreme Court.
- There is no pressure for change from the American people.

Major weaknesses

- It is more rigid than the uncodified UK constitution and is therefore less easily adapted, despite changing conditions (for example, the criticisms made of the Second Amendment, the right to bear arms).
- Many argue that too much power is given to unelected and unaccountable judges (though this is debatable).
- It can be argued that the growth of presidential and federal power has not been sufficiently constrained and that constitutional rights are therefore not sufficiently protected.
- The difficulties of governing in a separated and checked-and-balanced system can result in gridlock, where decisions are hard to make and carry out.

The American Constitution remains the 'political bible' of the USA, and is deeply revered by its citizens. Constitutionalism suffuses the daily operations of US government, and presidents at their inauguration say they will 'protect and defend' it.

The Constitution is the underlying feature of all the following pages in this section of the guide and of most examination questions. You are highly advised to read it before attempting any serious study of US government.

The US Constitution and federalism

Constitutions can be federal or unitary. The origins of the US Constitution as a federal constitution lay in the Articles of Confederation (which governed the USA from 1781 to 1788) and in the debates that took place over where power should be located. The key issue was whether power should be with the new federal (central) government or whether it should be with the individual states.

Like the separation of powers in the branches of government, federalism fragments power between the layers of government and avoids its concentration. It has, however, led to power struggles and controversy over where the balance of power should lie.

What is federalism?

Federalism involves the division of power between the national (federal) government and the 50 individual states. It is the decentralisation of power, with power dispersed between the two levels. It is sometimes referred to as 'dual sovereignty', as each of the 50 states also has its own government structured around:

- a State Constitution
- a State Governor (executive)

- a bicameral State House and Senate (legislature) — except Nebraska, which has a unicameral legislature
- a State Supreme Court (judiciary)

Federalism, in the words of Madison, avoids 'the danger of too much power in too few hands', thus helping to preserve freedom and adding another set of checks and balances on the exercise of political power.

The key benefit of federalism is that it maintains national unity while at the same time preserving state diversity. It also means, however, that American citizens are subject to two sets of laws that act directly upon them.

What does the Constitution say about federalism?

There is no mention of the word 'federalism' in the US Constitution, which was a compromise between the federalists, who wanted a strong national government, and the anti-federalists, who wanted power to lie with the individual states. However:

- the Constitution gives the states equal representation in the Senate (two per state)
- the Constitution specifies that an amendment can pass only with the agreement of three-quarters of the states
- the Tenth Amendment guarantees states' rights through the reserved powers (see below)

How does federalism work?

The Constitution gives both the federal and the state governments guaranteed powers and their own areas of authority, thus inviting a second struggle between the two layers of government, as well as between the branches within them.

There have been numerous developments in federalism since the Constitution was written in 1787:

- The **enumerated powers** (Article 1) state that the federal Congress can legislate on defence, currency and naturalisation of citizens, regulate interstate commerce and provide for the 'common defense'.
- The **inherent powers**, including responsibility for foreign relations and waging war, are also given to the federal government.
- The **implied powers** are not explicit but are shown in the Constitution's wording, for example that Congress can make laws that are 'necessary and proper' for exercising the enumerated powers and to provide for 'the general welfare'.
- In the *McCulloch v Maryland* **(1819)** case, the Supreme Court established the supremacy of the federal government and Congress over state governments through its interpretation of the 'necessary and proper' clause over the issue of a national bank. The Court's interpretation paved the way for later rulings upholding federal over state power.
- The **Sixteenth Amendment** in 1913 allowed for a federal income tax to be levied by the federal government across all the states. This was a watershed in the

development of federalism and federal government control of taxing and spending for federal policies and the subsequent dependence of the states on federal finance.

- The **reserved powers** are those left to the states and guaranteed by the Tenth Amendment. They form the basis of states' rights, such as law enforcement and electoral law, and explain the different laws in different states.
- The **concurrent powers** are those shared by both state and federal government, such as legislative power, taxation power, health, education and safety.

Phases of federalism

The parameters of federal and state power are not fixed and the nature of federal–state relations has developed and changed throughout US history. There have been several phases of federalism:

- **Dual federalism.** Before the 1930s New Deal, the federal and state governments were largely independent, with clearly defined spheres of influence and power rarely overlapping. This is referred to as a 'layer-cake', with separate and distinct layers.
- **Cooperative federalism.** This came after the huge expansion of federal government intervention and regulation after the Great Depression and subsequent New Deal. The term refers to the partnership that evolved between the two levels of government, with the federal government assisting the states to cope with the new demands: a national crisis demanded a centralised response. This was also true of the period of the Great Society under Lyndon Johnson's administration of the 1960s, when money was given to the states but with strings attached, so there was more control by the federal government. This phase of federalism is sometimes referred to as a 'marble cake', with an inseparable mix of layers.
- **New federalism.** This came about as a result of the Republican presidencies of Nixon and Reagan, as a reaction against the growth of federal government power and its bureaucratic costs. New federalism emphasised states' rights, small government and 'getting government off the backs of the people'. Both Republican administrations provided block grants to the states to spend as they wished (rather than having the states be directed in their spending by the requirements of the federal government through categorical grants). This continued into the presidency of Clinton, who famously declared that the 'era of big government is over' after the Republican takeover of Congress in 1994.
- The George W. Bush presidency started with a philosophy of small government and, Bush being an ex-governor, a commitment to states' rights. However, the demands of the war on terror, homeland security, the aftermath of Hurricane Katrina, and the No Child Left Behind Act resulted in more federal government intervention than would normally be seen in a Republican administration.

Where power *should* be is a question without an answer. Those who say it should be with the federal government (mainly liberals) favour strong decisive action and equality of provision across the states. Those who say it should be with the states (mainly conservatives) favour local autonomy and decision making close to the people. It is safe to say that the relationship between the federal government and the states remains complex, especially in a time of budget constraints and rising deficits.

What are the main advantages of federalism?

It is said that, in the USA, 'all politics is local', which is hardly surprising in a country so large and diverse. US federalism has many advantages:
- It provides an additional set of checks and balances on the exercise of power, guarding against an overpowerful central government.
- It allows for the diversity and traditions of the 50 states to be reflected.
- It provides opportunities for citizens to be politically involved at local level.
- The states can be training grounds for national leadership. George W. Bush was the Governor of Texas; Clinton was the Governor of Arkansas. Obama was a State Senator and then US Senator for Illinois.
- States can show both autonomy and initiative. They can even be laboratories for experimental new policies to see if they work, for example caps on carbon emissions in New York and California or the use of education vouchers in Wisconsin.

What are the main disadvantages of federalism?

- Too much fragmentation of government can lead to gridlock. The states can also be obstructive and refuse to conform, for example the refusal of the southern states to de-segregate after the Brown decision in 1954, claiming that states' rights allowed them to refuse.
- The variety of state laws on, for example, abortion, gun ownership and the death penalty causes confusion and a lack of cohesion in the country.
- There are significant economic inequalities between rich and poor states, such as Connecticut and Louisiana, and variable provisions for citizens, which only the federal government can equalise.
- There is democratic overload, with too many elective offices and, therefore, too many elections.

How federal is the USA in reality?

The history of the USA has seen a steady shift of power towards the federal government in Washington DC, which is probably inevitable in modern conditions. However, states still jealously guard their powers and their rights. The 'supremacy clause' of the Constitution ensures that federal government law prevails in a dispute and this has been upheld in several Supreme Court rulings over the implied powers (see p. 21).

The protection of rights in the US Constitution

The Founding Fathers were concerned above all to protect the rights and liberties of citizens under the new Constitution. Jefferson's Declaration of Independence focused on the 'inalienable rights' of the people and Madison felt that the Constitution as originally drafted did too little to protect citizens or the states against the potential tyranny of an overpowerful government. Many states were unlikely to ratify the new constitution without the inclusion of a Bill of Rights.

The Bill of Rights

These first ten amendments to the Constitution were ratified by the states in 1791 and have remained as they were since that date. They are entrenched and guaranteed constitutional rights:

- The **First Amendment** protects freedom of religion, the press, speech and assembly. It begins 'Congress shall make no law' abridging these freedoms. Freedom of speech has been interpreted as the freedom to burn the flag and to spend money to support political views.
- The **Second Amendment** protects the right to bear arms. This remains controversial but upheld.
- The **Third Amendment** protects the rights of property owners, including a broader protection of privacy.
- The **Fourth Amendment** guarantees freedom from unreasonable searches and seizures of persons and property.
- The **Fifth Amendment** guarantees the rights of the accused and includes the 'due process clause', whereby no person shall be deprived of life, liberty or property without due process of law. It also protects the right to silence in a court of law.
- The **Sixth Amendment** sets out rights for those standing trial and protects against arbitrary arrest and imprisonment.
- The **Seventh Amendment** deals mainly with civil law suits.
- The **Eighth Amendment** bans 'cruel and unusual punishment', which is controversial, given the existence of the death penalty in many states.
- The **Ninth Amendment** is concerned with the rights 'reserved to the people' and states that people may have other rights not found in the Bill of Rights. It has been used in many privacy cases, including *Roe* v *Wade*.
- The **Tenth Amendment** is concerned with the rights reserved to the states.

Rights are also protected by several of the other constitutional amendments, such as the Fourteenth Amendment with its reference to the 'equal protection of the laws'.

For the role of the Supreme Court in protecting constitutional rights through constitutional interpretation and judicial review, see pp. 59–60. In general, 'activist' courts protect and extend rights through interpretation, while courts that are more 'restrained' are less likely to do so. Remember that the interpretation of the Constitution by the Supreme Court can change over time. As we see later, this may depend on the composition and the prevailing judicial philosophy of the court.

It is important to note the existence of a strong 'rights culture' in the USA, with most Americans knowing their rights and understanding that the courts are there to protect them.

However, 'words on paper' do not always guarantee that these rights will be applied at all times and under all conditions. There are many instances in US history where rights have not been fully protected and applied:

- the denial of voting rights and civil rights to black Americans after the Fourteenth and Fifteenth amendments, when segregation and Jim Crow laws prevailed in the southern states
- the internment (imprisonment without trial) of Japanese Americans during the Second World War
- the passage of the Patriot Act, a raft of anti-terrorism measures such as wire tapping and electronic surveillance, passed by Congress after 9/11 — many argued such measures undermined constitutional rights, but they were not declared 'unconstitutional' by the Supreme Court
- the existence of Guantánamo Bay camp, where prisoners were detained without habeas corpus rights or 'due process of law' as a result of the so-called war on terror

It can therefore be argued that what happens to rights, despite constitutional protection, depends on the climate and events of the times.

Some comparisons with the UK constitution

The UK has a very different history from the USA, which explains many of the differences in the constitutional settlements. Whereas the American Constitution emerged after a revolutionary war of independence and the need to set up a new state, the UK constitution evolved gradually and organically through the ages without major upheavals and with no major design. As a result, the UK constitution is quite different from that of the USA in its provisions.

What are the main features of the UK constitution?

- There is no single, authoritative, codified document that is *the* constitution. However, the UK constitution cannot be described as unwritten, as there are many written elements to it. These include:
  - constitutional statutes, such as the 1911 and 1949 Parliament Acts, various Representation of the People Acts and the constitutional changes passed by the Labour Government after 1997, for example devolution of power
  - constitutional documents such as Magna Carta (1215)
  - authoritative writings such as Bagehot's *The English Constitution* (1867) or Dicey's writings on the rule of law
  - European treaties that the UK has signed up to, such as Maastricht
- The unwritten elements of the UK constitution include the following:
  - common law, such as royal prerogative powers, now largely exercised by the prime minister (but which can be changed by parliamentary statute)
  - the constitutional conventions — unwritten rules or practices based on custom and practice, which are regarded as binding but which cannot be enforced. They include some of the key practices in UK government, such as ministerial responsibility or cabinet government. Conventions can be changed by parliamentary statute.
- The main principle of the UK constitution is parliamentary sovereignty, as opposed to the constitutional sovereignty found in the USA. There is no higher authority than Parliament and no higher law. Any law can be made or unmade here with no challenge from any other body. There are no 'unconstitutional' laws.
- There is a fusion of powers in the UK system of government, with the executive being drawn from the legislature and also responsible to it (a parliamentary executive). As a result, there are fewer checks and balances in the UK system.
- The UK is a constitutional monarchy, not a republic.
- The UK constitution is often described as flexible or unentrenched because it can easily be changed through a law passed by a simple majority in Parliament. There is no need for complicated amendment procedures, and so it is easily adaptable to changing conditions and circumstances.
- There is a unitary rather than a federal system of government. Power is centralised and concentrated in the sovereign Westminster Parliament. Parliament can devolve power, as it did to Scotland and to a lesser degree Wales, and Parliament can take any devolved powers back again, as it did in Northern Ireland. (Note that in both cases it devolved power, not sovereignty.) Parliament can also bring the UK out of the European Union if ever there is a majority in Parliament to do so.
- Rights are not entrenched or guaranteed in the UK. There is no equivalent of the Bill of Rights. Parliament did pass the Human Rights Act in 1998 (in force in 2000), incorporating the European Convention of Human Rights into UK law, but the only challenge that can be made by judges if they think that a new law contravenes the convention is to issue a 'declaration of incompatibility'. They cannot strike down the law using judicial review, as the Supreme Court can do in the USA if a law contravenes any part of the Constitution. Similarly, the UK government can

'derogate' from the convention in order to pass an Act that contravenes the provisions of the Human Rights Act.

Advantages of the uncodified UK constitution

- Flexibility and adaptability to change as political circumstances change, without upheaval
- Use of referendums, as and when required, to legitimise constitutional change
- Stability of the system: deeply held traditions not requiring codification
- Strong and effective government carrying out mandates without gridlock and responding quickly in a crisis

Disadvantages of the uncodified UK constitution

- Lack of clarity as to what the constitution actually is
- Lack of entrenched and fully guaranteed rights
- No limits to Parliament's legislative power
- 'Executive dominance' and 'elective dictatorship': lack of effective checks and balances to a government with a large majority in the Commons
- Weakness of the constitutional conventions, which can be ignored as there are no sanctions (apart from public opinion and the media) if they are broken. One example is the decline of individual ministerial responsibility.
- Any constitutional change in the UK has tended to be tinkering or piecemeal, with no fundamental constitutional overhaul of the way the country is governed.

The legislative branch of government: US Congress

The US Congress is the legislative branch of the federal government and its role is described in Article 1 of the Constitution. This shows the clear intention of the framers of the Constitution that Congress was to have a dominant role. The Constitution gives all legislative power to Congress to make laws for the USA, although today, because of vastly changed conditions, it tends to follow a presidential agenda.

Congress may be the most powerful legislature in the world, but it operates under a codified constitution, with separated powers from the other branches of government and checks and balances to limit its powers. Its legislative powers are also constrained by the Bill of Rights, with the First Amendment starting 'Congress shall make no law', as befits the framers' desire for limited government.

Congress has been described as a policy-making rather than a policy-influencing legislature. This is unusual, as most modern legislatures are executive dominated.

Why is the US Congress so powerful?

- It is independent from the executive branch of government and cannot be controlled by it.
- It is not dominated by party, as many modern legislatures are.
- It is the representative assembly of the USA, the voices of the people.
- It has many constitutional powers, both enumerated and implied.

Bicameralism

Congress is made up of two different but equally powerful houses, the **House of Representatives** and the **Senate**. The Constitution deliberately created two houses that would check and balance each other and respond in different ways to different constituencies and pressures.

Different representation

The House of Representatives represents districts within states. There are 435 districts and they are apportioned according to the population of the state: the more populous the state, the greater the number of districts within it. California, at the time of writing the state with the largest population, has 53 districts; in small states with low population density, like South Dakota, the state *is* the district. However, this may change after the 2010 census, as states can gain or lose districts according to population change. Re-districting is done by partisan state legislatures and is often controversial because of gerrymandering (altering the boundaries for party advantage).

The Senate represents the states. Because of the Connecticut Compromise, there is equal representation of the states, with two Senators per state regardless of size or population. After the Seventeenth Amendment in 1913, Senators were directly elected by the people rather than indirectly elected by state legislatures, bringing more democratic legitimacy to their role. However, this representation has been criticised as unfair as, for example, Wyoming (population less than 500,000) has the same Senate representation as California (population 37 million).

Different terms of office

The House of Representatives is elected for 2-year terms of office. The intention was to keep Representatives highly responsive to the wishes of the people, and the effect of these very short terms does make re-election their prime motivating force. The House is a more parochial chamber than the Senate, dominated by the constituency interests of the 'folks back home', and most House members 'vote their district'.

Senators are elected for 6-year terms, but elections for the Senate are staggered, with a third of the Senators up for re-election every 2 years in both mid-term and presidential elections. The intention was that Senators would be more like national statesmen, above the fray, with a more long-term view on political issues compared to their more populist counterparts in the House. The longer terms of the Senators protect them from the 'whims of the day', and the fact that they represent states with a huge diversity of interests within them means that they are less parochial than the House Representatives in their voting.

Different status and prestige

The 100-member Senate is regarded as a more prestigious chamber of elder statesmen and nationally known figures, and is given more attention and status than the 435-member House. Many Representatives aspire to a Senate seat but not the other way round and most presidents have come from the Senate, rarely from the House.

The constitutional powers of the House and the Senate

The House and the Senate share some power. For example, the Constitution gives both houses:
- legislative power, including the power to override the presidential veto
- oversight power
- the power of the purse (taxation and spending power)
- the power to declare war
- the power to propose and pass constitutional amendments with a two-thirds majority
- a role in the impeachment process for 'high crimes and misdemeanors'. The House draws up the Articles of Impeachment and the Senate conducts the trial. Clinton was found not guilty at his impeachment trial in 1998 for perjury, and Nixon resigned before his likely impeachment in 1974 over Watergate
- a role if the Electoral College is deadlocked after a presidential election

However, the Constitution gave the House of Representatives the power to *originate* all money bills: for example, taxation is considered first in the House and then in the Senate. This gives the House the power to set the financial agenda and to control the purse strings of government through its powerful Ways and Means and Appropriations committees.

The Senate has significant constitutional powers denied to the House, such as the 'advice and consent' powers, giving it additional influence and oversight over the executive. These powers include:
- Confirmation with a simple majority of presidential appointments, such as Supreme Court justices, cabinet secretaries and ambassadors. The Senate has used these powers to deny a president's chosen nominee, for example the rejection of Reagan's choice of Bork for the Supreme Court in 1987 and George Bush's choice of Tower as defense secretary in 1989. However, presidents have overcome opposition at times by the use of recess appointments, such as with John Bolton as UN Ambassador in 2005.

- Ratification with a two-thirds majority of treaties that have been negotiated by the president, who is chief diplomat. This gives the Senate some power over US foreign policy, although presidents have often resorted to the use of executive agreements to avoid the need for Senate ratification as it has rejected several negotiated treaties, such as Versailles in 1919 and SALT II in 1979.

Internal workings/procedures of the two houses

The House, chaired by the Speaker, operates in a more formal and procedural way, with rules and limits on debate, as befits a chamber of 435 members.

The smaller Senate, chaired by the vice-president, who can vote only to break a tied vote, has procedures that are more informal and less rule-bound. The Senate has a tradition of unlimited debate, which gives rise to the infamous Senate filibuster (discussed on p. 31).

Both House and Senate members are involved in:
- committees and subcommittees, both permanent and ad hoc
- pork-barrelling, or 'bringing home the bacon', on spending bills
- 'log-rolling' (vote trading on bills)
- coalition building to gain a majority of votes
- party and congressional caucuses

There are relatively weak party ties, although there is some evidence that these are increasing, and all Senators and Representatives try to avoid alienating strong lobbies, who seek access to them and their decision making.

Congress and legislation

The legislative process in Congress is frequently described as an obstacle course. Words associated with it are often negative, such as 'block', 'pigeon hole', 'veto'. Only a small fraction of bills introduced in Congress actually pass and their failure is often unrelated to their merits, as in the case of healthcare reform or civil rights. Bills are especially vulnerable to defeat if they are controversial or opposed by powerful special interests. Furthermore, bills can be so significantly amended during the process that they become unrecognisable.

However, there *are* circumstances where bills have passed easily without being mired in the legislative labyrinth. An example is the Patriot Act, passed on a wave of patriotism and deference to the commander-in-chief after 9/11.

How is legislation initiated in the USA?

Legislation can only be initiated by a member of Congress (all members have legislative initiative), although most legislation today originates from a presidential agenda, with policy goals outlined in the president's State of the Union Address in January. This is followed by the presidential budget, which must be passed by both houses. However, although the 'President proposes', 'Congress disposes' — all legislative proposals have to be introduced by a member of each house and must pass through both houses concurrently. There is no guarantee that legislation or the budget will pass in the way the president wishes it to, especially if there is divided government and presidential–congressional relations are poor, or if the houses have different party majorities.

Why is the legislative process so difficult?

The main reason for legislative failure is the number of veto points in both the House and the Senate where a bill may fail:

- House standing committee stage. Most bills die here as they are pigeon-holed by the chair, thus taken off the committee's agenda for the session.
- House subcommittee stage. Here the bill is examined in detail in hearings, with evidence taken from interested parties such as lobbyists or executive branch officials. The bill can be significantly amended at this stage, as pork-barrelling occurs, with numerous amendments or riders added to the bill to benefit constituents or special interests. The bill can fail at this stage.
- House Rules Committee. This powerful committee decides whether to give time to the bill on the floor of the House for debate. If this is not given, the bill dies.
- Floor debate. The amended bill is debated by the whole chamber. Log-rolling, the exchange of votes and trading of favours by Representatives may occur. Although there are whips and some ideological voting, there is little party discipline and most members are more mindful of the folks back home or special interests in the roll-call voting at the end of the debate. The bill may fail on this floor vote.
- The bill follows similar stages in the Senate. It may fail in debate here due to a filibuster, the classic legislative delaying tactic whereby Senators can individually or collectively 'talk out' a bill to defeat it. The filibuster is used because of the unlimited debate that is allowed and is a jealously guarded tactic employed by both parties when they are in a minority position in the Senate. Since 1975 it has been possible to end a filibuster through 'cloture', but this needs 60 votes, which are hard to gain, so defeat can come here. The bill can also fail in a vote at the end of Senate debate.
- Because the bill passes through both houses concurrently, it is likely that a different bill will emerge from both. The two different bills will need to be reconciled so an agreed bill can be sent to the White House. This is done through a Conference Committee, where Senators and Representatives try to reach a consensus through bargaining and compromise. If this cannot be done, then the bill dies.
- If reconciled, the bill needs to go back to both chambers for a final simple majority vote. It can still die here in either chamber.

Because of the separation of powers and checks and balances, the bill has to be signed by the president to become federal law. The president may veto the whole bill (he has no 'line-item veto' to turn down just the parts he doesn't like, as this was declared unconstitutional in 1998). If the veto is not overridden by a two-thirds vote in both houses and the veto is sustained, then the bill fails. Clinton vetoed 32 bills in his two terms, only two of which were subject to a congressional override. A president may 'pocket veto' a bill, which means he ignores it; if near the end of a congressional session, the bill will die.

Even if the bill becomes law it can still be challenged in the courts, and the Supreme Court, using its power of judicial review, can declare it (or its parts) to be unconstitutional and therefore void.

Key points regarding the legislative process in Congress

- The separation of powers and numerous checks and balances make the process of law making difficult.
- The built-in tensions between the two houses and between Congress and president, as they are elected separately with few shared mandates, often lead to gridlock.
- The absence of strong party loyalty or effective party discipline may lead to a lack of party unity on votes. Clinton's healthcare bill was defeated in 1994 even with a Democratic Congress.
- Coalitions have to be built on each separate bill to construct a majority of votes. The president has only the power to persuade, through his Congressional Liaison Office.
- Congress blocks legislation on the president's agenda more effectively than it provides an alternative agenda of its own.
- Members of Congress pork-barrel in order to provide projects in their districts or states to help their re-election. They are less effective in providing a long-term or national perspective on policy, unless there is a major event such as 9/11 or the 2008 banking crisis.

All these factors lead to criticisms of the legislative process in the US Congress.

However, in its defence, it does avoid the criticisms of executive dominance and elective dictatorship found in the UK. The process means there is a need to compromise and reach a consensus before the successful passage of federal law.

Congressional oversight

This is the power of Congress to scrutinise and check the activities of the executive branch of government. Although the Constitution does not explicitly give this power to Congress, it is exercised through:

- the legislative process
- Congress's control of the purse strings of government
- the Senate's advice and consent powers
- the impeachment process

When the federal government was small, oversight was relatively unimportant. However, it is now one of the main functions of Congress in conditions of big and complex government.

Congressional committees

Oversight is done through the powerful permanent standing committees and is made even more effective by the huge number of congressional staff and resources devoted to oversight on Capitol Hill, such as the Congressional Budget Office.

All legislatures have committee systems within them, drawn from the larger body and with specific responsibilities. It is often said that the floors of the chambers are for debating, while the smaller committees are for working. As Woodrow Wilson said in 1884, 'Congressional government is committee government: Congress in its committee rooms is Congress at work.'

Why are the congressional committees so powerful?

- They have a key role in the legislative process, reviewing all bills in their area, with power to pigeon-hole, amend or block.
- Their permanence means they develop policy specialisation and expertise, which balances that of the executive branch.
- They conduct public hearings and have extensive oversight powers over cabinet secretaries or agency heads, with power to subpoena witnesses.
- They have close links with the federal departments and agencies that they oversee and finance, and also with pressure groups. These links are called 'iron triangles' and can dominate areas of policy making. An example would be the relationships between the 'military-industrial complex' of the Pentagon, the armed services committees and defence contractors.
- The 'blue ribbon' committees are especially important. Examples include those dealing with taxation (Ways and Means) and spending (Appropriations or Senate Finance) and those with influence in foreign policy, such as Senate Foreign Relations. The Judiciary Committee conducts confirmation hearings for Supreme Court justices. The House Rules Committee can block legislation.

How is membership of congressional committees decided?

Members of committees are chosen by the party committees, and membership is according to party strength. The chairs of the committees are very powerful and always come from the majority party. Most members of Congress want committee assignments affecting their constituency interests, where they can effectively pork-barrel. Representatives from farming districts and states will want to be on the Agriculture Committee, while those representing urban districts will want to be a member of a committee dealing with urban affairs. David Mayhew, in his book on Congress, calls this 'home style activities'. Members 'claim credit' for their committee activities in their re-election campaigns (which their challengers cannot do).

How important is the role of party in Congress?

British government is described as party government and the House of Commons as party-dominated, with strong party loyalty and discipline within it. Disraeli was famous for the instruction to his MPs in Parliament to 'damn your principles and stick to your party'. In the US Congress the advice would be to 'damn your party and stick to your district'.

Congress has a relatively weak party system within it, and members of Congress are relatively independent of strong party ties, but the key word here is 'relatively'.

One reason for the relative lack of party influence is the way that members of Congress are elected. Although all are elected with a party label (apart from a few Independents), they will generally raise their own campaign finance, which is not legally restricted. They also run their own personalised election campaigns based on their individual views and the views prevalent in their districts or states. They have been described as 'independent political entrepreneurs' for this reason. When they have achieved success through their own personal efforts they do not feel beholden to their party for their election. As a result, there has been relatively little party cohesion, with each House member and Senator more attuned to their voters' wishes than to their party ties.

Many members of Congress do have their own ideological views on issues, whether liberal, conservative or moderate, and this influences the way they vote in roll call votes. But this does not necessarily (or always) coincide with voting with their party.

The USA used to have no equivalent of manifestos or clear mandates, and this perhaps hampered the development of the sort of party cohesion found in the UK. In the 1994 mid-term elections, however, House Republicans ran on a de facto manifesto called the 'Contract with America', containing a clear reform agenda that they were all committed to support, although little of this was successfully enacted.

Finally, there *is* some degree of party linkage found in both houses, with the majority of Republicans voting against a majority of Democrats on most issues.

Party influence

Apart from the leadership role in Congress of the committee chairs, there are also majority- and minority-party leaders in both houses. There is also the House Speaker who is, in effect, a party leader and the link between the power centres in Congress. They all serve to provide some degree of party unity and organisation.

There are also whips, who try to achieve party cohesion in votes. However, they are limited in their efforts, as there are no carrots of office that can be used to influence members' behaviour and no sticks of discipline to use against rebels voting against their party.

To some extent, legislative success depends on the persuasion skills of the party power brokers, for example the famous 'Johnson treatment' applied by LBJ to fellow Senators when he was Senate majority leader in the 1950s. Success can also depend on the power of persuasion of the White House incumbent.

In effect, there is little that can be done to persuade members to vote with their party if they do not wish to. Most votes are bipartisan and there are 'shifting coalitions' of votes on different issues. In the past, the highly conservative southern democrats were rare voters with their party, and many moderate Republicans in recent times did not always vote with their party on social and economic issues.

However, although lacking the party loyalty, discipline and leadership of the UK House of Commons with clear party manifestos and mandates, party membership still provides the best predictor of the vote in both houses of Congress.

Growing party cohesion/partisanship in Congress

There is some evidence of growing party cohesion as a result of the more ideolog-ical politics of the Reagan era and its legacy of more coherent ideological conser-vatism. This was particularly evident in the 'Contract with America' and in the speakership of Newt Gingrich and his successor Dennis Hastert, along with the House Republican majority leader Tom DeLay. DeLay was nicknamed 'The Hammer' for his iron discipline and skill in 'nailing down' the legislation wanted by President Bush after 2001.

The Democratic Party became ideologically more liberal and cohesive in response, helped by the loss of its southern, conservative wing through electoral defeats or by defections in Congress. This led to more party voting and party unity on votes, but nowhere near the level seen in the House of Commons.

Some members of Congress will vote with their party over 90% of the time, others much less so. In general, members of Congress will vote with their party unless there are significant constituency pressures on them not to do so. Otherwise, the folks back home in the district or state are the most important influence on roll call votes, which are recorded and can be published back in the district or used by pressure groups.

Pressure groups

Pressure groups and their lobbyists seek access to members of Congress and become active on all issues affecting their interests, for example the NRA (National Rifle Association) on gun law reform, or the AARP (American Association of Retired People) on Medicare or prescription drug charges. They can gain access and influence by helping to fund campaigns or because they are representing millions of voters that members of Congress do not want to alienate. Members of Congress also wish to avoid being targeted for electoral defeat if they speak out against powerful lobbies in the USA.

The White House

Do not forget the influence of the White House and the president's congressional liaison team. Presidential persuasion may be effective or not. There may be helpful party linkages; for example, President Obama has Democrat majorities in both the Senate and the House and he is an ex-Senator and therefore a Washington insider, used to the ways of Congress. President Bush, an ex-governor, struggled in his last two lame-duck years to get any agreement from Congress for his political agenda.

The congressional caucuses

These are cross-party coalitions of members of Congress who share the same or similar ideology, ethnicity or regional interests. Examples include the black caucus (all Democrat), who vote and act together on issues relating to the specific interests of black Americans, such as affirmative action, and the Hispanic caucus uniting on immigration policy.

Congress and representation

In addition to its legislative and oversight functions, Congress is the representative assembly for the USA. Both houses of Congress have a function of representation of the views and interests of the people in their districts and states. This is given the highest priority by members of Congress, who take their role as 'representatives of the people' more seriously than most other democratically elected representatives.

Congressional elections

These take place every 2 years, when all the Representatives and one-third of the Senate are elected. The elections tend to be fought around local issues rather than national ones, and there is a 'locality rule' that those standing for election should be residents of the state or district they represent, thus strengthening the idea that 'all politics is local'.

In elections, members of Congress stress their commitment to constituency service rather than loyalty to party, leading to a very high re-election rate (over 90%). It is argued that the incumbency advantage is now so great that congressional elections are no longer competitive in very 'safe' districts and states.

Why are incumbents re-elected?
The incumbency advantages of members of Congress include:
- their huge resources, such as staffs in the state or district as well as Washington and free mailing for publicity called the 'franking privilege'

- their name recognition and 'visibility' in the district or state, thanks to constant local media coverage
- their opportunities to serve their constituents' interests, such as 'bringing home the bacon' to their districts or states and then 'credit-claiming' for all they have done for their constituents while in Washington
- their huge campaign war chests from special interests and political action commit-tees who wish to gain access to them
- the gerrymandering of districts by partisan state legislatures to make them even more 'safe'
- the difficulties faced by any challengers of showing that they could provide a better service to constituents

However, it is still possible for challengers to beat incumbents with, for example:
- an anti-Washington 'kick the bums out' mood in the country, as in 1994 and 2008
- a particularly unpopular member of Congress targeted for defeat
- a huge campaign war chest to outspend the incumbent

But these circumstances are rare, and only 'open' seats provide real competition. It is paradoxical that Congress as an institution is highly unpopular in the USA, but most Americans support and vote for their incumbent Representative or Senator.

There have been calls for term limits on members but this would need a constitu-tional amendment, which successful incumbents are unlikely to propose in Congress.

Members of Congress and constituency service

The first Congress established that representatives should act as trustees for the whole nation, not as mere delegates of their constituents.

Today, however, the majority of members of Congress spend time on constituency rather than national service, through their successful pork-barrelling, which pleases their constituents but does little to reduce budget deficits or the national debt. Members of Congress are the link between their constituents and the huge and imper-sonal bureaucracies based in Washington, and they help their constituents with problems such as Medicare, veterans' programmes and tax issues. It is these 'home-style' activities that members of Congress can claim credit for — and often prioritise over trying to eliminate environmental pollution or bringing down inflation — and this is what secures their re-election.

Criticisms are made of members of Congress who appear too concerned with providing benefits to their home state or district, to the detriment of the national interest of the USA as a whole. However, when they get pork-barrel federally funded projects for their districts, they *are* representing their constituents, just as they are when they oppose progressive income taxes if they represent a wealthy district, or when they support them if they represent a poorer one. No one expects a black congresswoman representing a poor New York district to support subsidies for Montana wheat growers, but she would be expected to support welfare services for her district. Similarly, if funding for space or weapons programmes brings federal jobs to the home state, then the Senator should vote for them. Re-election is the true test of democracy, as this is the major check that voters have over their representatives and their behaviour in Congress.

What should a representative represent?

This is one of the key questions in political theory. There are no right answers here, only debate about the nature of representation. Should representatives represent those who sent them to Washington or the broader national interest?

One theory of representation was put forward by Edmund Burke, writing in the UK in the 1770s, who stated that elected representatives are trustees of their constituents and the nation. The Burkeian notion is that representatives are elected to exercise their judgement on behalf of those they represent, and they are not merely delegates of their constituents, mandated to speak for their interests alone. There is more to representative democracy than serving the immediate whims of constituents; representatives of the people should speak and vote for the good of the whole nation. According to Burke, a Congress full of representatives concerned with narrow constituency interests is not doing what a representative assembly should be doing. But it does appear to be what the US Congress is doing!

Congress is often perceived as a battlefield of different and competing interests, and members are put under pressure from their party, their constituents, special interest lobbies, the executive branch, their own conscience and the 'national interest'. The Constitution's 'invitation to struggle' to the branches of government has become a reality. The result, however, is often an inability to find solutions to America's problems, whether social, economic or foreign, and a lack of a coherent national policy from 535 individuals pursuing local interests and demands. This is the problem faced by the president, leading the executive branch of government, who has a national perspective and a national constituency, but who also has to persuade the individualistic and fragmented Congress to support him, which is not easy to do.

The social background of members of Congress

No elected representatives are completely socially representative of the people that they represent. There are no 'representative democracies' in this social sense. The

UK Parliament is not a social microcosm or mirror image of the nation and the same is true of the US Congress. Despite the huge social, economic, ethnic, racial and religious diversity of the American people, the Congress does not 'look like them'. This does not fit with the resemblance model of representation, as Congress is largely 'white, male, middle class and middle aged' and dominated by lawyers and other professionals.

However, anyone can stand for Congress if they fulfil the constitutional age, citizenship and residence requirements. There are no formal barriers to a more socially representative Congress. It is more diverse now than in the past, with more women and ethnic minority members. This is due to factors such as:

- the changing role of women generally and the growth of political action committees (PACs) supporting women candidates, such as Emily's List
- growing black and Hispanic activism and political involvement
- the impact of majority-minority districts (districts with a black or Hispanic majority)

Why is Congress socially unrepresentative?

- 'Ordinary people' or women, young or minority candidates do not want to be representatives and do not put themselves forward even if they did.
- The perceived need for high levels of education and skills for a political career acts as a disincentive.
- The need for large campaign war chests excludes those who are not millionaires or those without access to the money needed to run.
- There is a perception that politics is an occupation for rich, white males or for political dynasties such as the Kennedys or Bushes.

However, questions arise as to whether a legislature has to be socially representative as well as politically representative. Do you have to be a woman to speak and vote on women's issues? How socially representative does it have to be? Does it really matter that legislatures are not socially representative? How could a legislature be made to be more socially representative and a social microcosm of the nation? The debate on these questions will continue.

Comparisons with the bicameral Westminster Parliament

- The UK has a parliamentary system of government.
- Parliament operates under an uncodified constitution but follows rules laid down by constitutional statutes, such as the 1911 and 1949 Parliament Acts, and various constitutional conventions that have evolved — for example, that a government defeated on a vote of no confidence in the House of Commons resigns.

- There are no fixed terms of office, apart from a 5-year limit on parliamentary terms, and no separate elections for the executive and legislature.
- There is a fusion of executive and legislative powers and the prime minister and cabinet are drawn from the majority party in Parliament, claiming an electoral mandate to carry out their legislative and policy agenda. As a result, there are fewer effective challenges to the power of the executive from the legislature; the UK system is described as being 'executive dominated' and Parliament as being a policy-influencing rather than a policy-making legislature.
- The government is responsible to Parliament, and it answers to the House of Commons through procedures such as question time or through the select committee system. The Commons can remove the executive through a successful vote of no confidence, as in 1979.
- There is party dominance of the legislature based on:
  - the party majority in the Commons and on the standing and select committees
  - the carrot of promotion to ministerial office
  - the stick of party discipline, including whip withdrawal and refusal to select as a parliamentary candidate for the party

The result is that the UK Parliament is often described as 'little more than a talking shop' and MPs seen as 'lobby fodder'.

However, it is argued that the government is strong and effective and can take decisions easily, thus avoiding legislative gridlock. It will then answer for these decisions at the next general election.

Parliament and legislation

- Apart from the occasional backbench rebellion, the government can pass its legislation quickly through the houses.
- Any opposition from the House of Lords can be overcome with the use of the 1949 Parliament Act or the Salisbury Convention.
- Royal Assent is automatic.

Parliament and scrutiny

- Question time is not effective for adequate scrutiny of the government.
- The standing legislative committees are weak in the scrutiny of legislation as they lack permanence and expertise.
- The select scrutiny committees are regarded as toothless watchdogs compared to their US equivalent, lacking the power and resources to effectively scrutinise.

Control of finance

- The Budget passes easily through the House of Commons. Amendments are impossible without the agreement of the government. There are no opportunities for pork-barrelling.
- Because of the 1911 Parliament Act, the Budget does not go to the House of Lords.

Representation

- The House of Commons is the representative assembly but, with 4–5 year terms of office, MPs do not see representation as their main role. Strong party loyalty and manifesto commitments protect them against constituency or special interest pressure. Most see their main role as being a party representative, supporting policies based on party ideology and finance.
- The House of Commons is not socially representative of the UK population, although there have been attempts to make its composition more diverse with all-women shortlists.
- The House of Lords is unelected, with life peers, Church of England bishops, a rump of 92 hereditary peers and (until 2009–10) the Law Lords. It cannot be defended democratically, but paradoxically it is more socially representative than the Commons. It has also successfully challenged the government in many policy areas, such as the 2008 proposals for 42-day detention. As a result, it is often regarded as a better protector of civil liberties than the more party- and government-dominated lower chamber.

The executive branch of government

The executive is the core of government, where policy is formed and executed. It provides the political leadership of the country. Article 2 of the Constitution sets out:
- the popular election of the president through the medium of the Electoral College with a fixed term of 4 years
- the restriction of the president to two terms of office (Twenty-second Amendment)
- the only possible removal of the president by a successful impeachment and trial by the House and Senate
- the specific constitutional powers of the president

It is the formal separation of powers and resulting checks and balances that distinguish the US presidential system of government from the parliamentary system found in the UK. The political scientist Neustadt argued that, in the 'separated system of shared powers', the power of the president becomes only the 'power to persuade', which includes bargaining and compromise with the legislative branch of government. Neustadt's views became the accepted model of presidential power.

He also argued that the office of president was one of inherent weakness rather than strength, and that the powers of the president were no guarantee that power could actually be exercised. In his view, presidential leadership was possible only when there were presidents of extraordinary temperament and experience and in extraordinary crisis conditions such as depression or war. F. D. Roosevelt is often given as the best example of such a president.

The US president is usually seen as the most powerful person in the world, but the Constitution restricts the use of executive power, especially in domestic policy, by several means.

The paradox of the US presidency is that despite the apparent omnipotence of the office, with huge expectations of it, there is much evidence of political weakness and many presidencies are characterised by disappointments and failure. This is expressed in terms such as the 'imperial presidency' or the 'imperilled presidency', used at different times and under different conditions.

The American presidency is a complex office, with presidents needing many political skills to exercise the constitutional powers granted to them. To some extent the study of the presidency is a study of the person holding the office, the individual's abilities and style, and the circumstances and events surrounding that particular presidency, as well as the office itself. To paraphrase the UK prime minister Asquith, 'The office of president is whatever the holder is able, or chooses, to make of it.' One of the enduring debates in US government is 'How powerful is the president?' As in other political debates, the usual answer is 'it depends'. Understanding context is therefore crucial.

What are the constitutional powers of the American president?

The Founding Fathers feared tyranny and an 'elective monarch' above all else, but they were ambivalent about the office of president. They gave the office powers, but also checked these powers, making executive power hard to wield. However, the statement 'all executive power shall be vested in a president of the United States of America' in Article 2 is particularly vague and has led to the stretching of the powers of the office by modern 'activist' presidents in particular, allowing flexibility in their exercise.

Formal, enumerated powers

The president's formal, enumerated constitutional powers are as follows:
- **Chief executive.** Executive power is given *only* to the president. The executive branch of government and its coordination are under the president's control and he is responsible for the federal budget, setting out the policy agenda for the USA. Executive powers also include the powers of patronage and pardon.
- **Commander-in-chief.** The president is leader of the US armed forces and responsible for their deployment.
- **Chief diplomat.** The Constitution gives the president the power to make treaties with other countries, although increasingly presidents use 'executive agreements', thus avoiding the need for Senate ratification.

However, these formal constitutional powers are checked and balanced by the independent powers granted to Congress in Article 1 of the Constitution.

How have presidential roles developed since the Constitution was written?

The office of president today is very different from that envisaged by the framers of the Constitution in 1787 — the circumstances that have given rise to modern presidential power could not have been foreseen.

Implied roles and powers

The modern presidency has developed new implied roles and powers that are not in the codified Constitution:

- **Chief legislator.** Although the president has no formal legislative power, most legislation is initiated in the executive branch and presented to Congress in the annual State of the Union Address. The president is not guaranteed to see his legislative proposals enacted into law, but he does have the constitutional power of the regular veto and can exercise a pocket veto at the end of a congressional session (see p. 32). Use of the veto, however, is usually a sign of presidential weakness as it demonstrates that he has failed to persuade Congress to pass legislative proposals in the way he wants. He is forced to veto all the legislation, including some things that he wants, because he lacks the power of a line-item veto. This was denied by the Supreme Court as it granted legislative power to the executive.
- **World leader.** The president has huge international status and 'treads the world stage'. This has been particularly the case since the Cold War and the dominance of foreign policy.
- **Party leader.** Although not elected as a party leader in the UK sense, the president is seen as a partisan figure. However, as Clinton found out with the defeat of his healthcare proposals in 1994, he cannot command or even rely on the support of his party in Congress.
- **Head of state.** The president is the only national symbol and the focal point for loyalty. As well as being a political leader, he performs the kind of ceremonial and symbolic functions performed by the queen in the UK as head of state, in effect combining the two roles.

Two factors in particular have allowed the stretching of the power of the office:

- The presidency is the only institution of US government capable of acting quickly and decisively in a crisis, so providing leadership for the country.
- The president is the only nationally elected politician speaking for the national interest within a fragmented system of government.

However, the balance of power between the president and Congress is not fixed but fluid, and changes with circumstances and events. The ebbs and flows tend to be characterised by a pattern of:

- presidential dominance during times of economic or foreign policy crisis, such as during the Cold War or after 9/11
- congressional reassertion of power when the crisis is over

The presidency since the 1930s

The power of the modern presidency developed from the 1930s as a result of the growth of federal government intervention in the economy in response to economic depression. It further developed when America moved from an isolationist foreign policy to become the 'world's policeman' after the Second World War, which saw the growth of America's enormous military power and influence in the world. Foreign policy is now largely presidential territory and Congress has generally deferred to the White House in this area, as the nation rallies round the president during conflicts.

The Nixon presidency (1968–72 and 1972–74) was seen as the culmination of the growth of presidential power. The historian Schlesinger in 1973 called this the 'imperial presidency'. Presidential power, however, contained the possibility of the abuse of this power, and this was seen in presidential actions during the Vietnam War and executive abuses of power in the Watergate scandal.

The Congress, both during the Nixon presidency and after Watergate, reasserted its constitutional powers to become the 'resurgent Congress'. It increased its authority over the executive by:

- increasing congressional resources to make Congress more effective in oversight, such as the setting up of the Congressional Budget Office
- passing the Case Act of 1972, forcing the president to inform Congress of all executive agreements made with other states
- allowing the passage of the War Powers Resolution in 1973 (vetoed by Nixon but the veto was overridden), restricting, in theory at least, the president's powers to commit troops into hostilities
- passing the Budget and Impoundment Control Act in 1974 to prevent the president from impounding (i.e. not spending) money agreed by Congress
- the threat of impeachment, leading to the resignation of the 'imperial' Nixon in 1974

These factors led to new arguments as to whether the post-Watergate presidency (of Ford and Carter in particular) was now not 'imperial' but rather 'imperilled'. The additional constraints came on top of the traditional and long-standing restraints on the exercise of presidential power in the form of the following.

Congress

The House and the Senate individually or collectively have the power to:
- defeat the president's legislative proposals in the legislative process
- exercise full oversight over his actions and activities
- refuse to fund any of his proposals (even his budget was rejected in 1989 and 1995)
- refuse to confirm his appointments, ratify his treaties or declare war
- override his veto with a two-thirds majority in both houses
- impeach him for 'high crimes and misdemeanors'

The Supreme Court

Using the power of judicial review, the Supreme Court can declare the president's actions unconstitutional, as they did in the case of Nixon's claims of executive privilege over the Watergate tapes and in Truman's seizure of the steel mills during the Korean War. George W. Bush, in *Hamdan v Rumsfeld* (2006), saw his detention without trial of 'enemy combatants' ruled unconstitutional.

Public opinion and the mass media

The president needs public and media support to deal with Congress, and needs to win over hearts and minds. However, if the president's approval ratings are low, there will be little he can do against hostile public opinion, which will be reflected in increasingly influential and aggressive news media. This is often the case in the 'lame-duck period' at the end of the fixed two terms of office when there is no possibility of re-election and members of Congress are fixated on their own chances of being re-elected.

The president and domestic and foreign policy: 'two presidencies'

All presidents try to keep a high profile in foreign policy. This is because they all face difficulties in enacting domestic policy in areas such as health care or welfare, where there is little political consensus. Most leave office with little achievement in domestic policy. As a result, they tend to focus on their foreign-policy, commander-in-chief role in order to secure their legacy and reputation when they leave office. In foreign policy, Congress usually defers to the president's wishes and he is given a relatively free rein in pursuing his own agenda. This has been referred to as a 'bifurcated presidency' — weak in domestic policy, stronger in foreign.

Achieving legislative and policy goals

How can a president try to achieve his legislative and policy goals, given the 'separated institutions sharing power'? He can do so through a variety of means:
- by his power of persuasion or successful coalition-building skills
- by effective use of his Congressional Liaison Office in the West Wing
- by inviting to the White House or Camp David important members of Congress whose votes he needs

- by campaigning for the re-election of important members of Congress (if he is popular) or staying away (if unpopular)
- by using the media to appeal, over the head of Congress, to the public to support his proposals, as in Roosevelt's 'fireside chats' or modern TV appeals by presidents in a crisis. This is called the use of the 'bully pulpit' to inspire public support.

The success of the above methods will depend on several variables:
- whether the president is in his 'honeymoon' (usually the first 100 days or the first year of office) or 'lame-duck' final period of office when power is ebbing away
- whether he is in the first or second term of office
- whether or not he has clear priorities, leadership vision and a governing strategy
- whether his public approval ratings are high or low (Bush's were 26% at the end of his second term but over 90% after 9/11)
- whether he has long electoral 'coat-tails', and therefore majorities of his own party in both houses of Congress, or no coat-tails and therefore divided party government. The latter is often the case after the mid-terms, as Clinton experienced in 1994 with the Republican takeover of Congress.
- whether or not he has a strong mandate. President Obama was elected with 53% of the popular vote in 2008 but Clinton managed only 43% in 1992.
- whether he is a Washington insider (ex-Senators) or outsider (ex-governors) and skilled or unskilled in the ways of Washington
- whether or not he has good political and leadership skills
- the events and circumstances that dominate his presidency. In times of crisis, as we have seen, both the Congress and the Supreme Court tend to defer to the president as he 'wraps himself in the flag' in a wave of national patriotism.

Examples can be found of all the above variables in the studies of different presidents and presidencies and their relationships with Congress at different times and under differing circumstances and events. Such examples include: Kennedy and the Cuban Missile Crisis; Johnson and Vietnam and civil rights; Nixon and China and Watergate; Carter and energy and the Arab–Israeli peace process; Reagan and the end of the Cold War, but also rising deficits; Bush Senior and the first Gulf War, but also recession; Clinton and economic boom, but also his impeachment; George W. Bush and 9/11, Hurricane Katrina and the Iraq war.

A new 'imperial presidency'?

The aftermath of 9/11 and the subsequent war on terror, which came to dominate the political agenda, saw more concentration of power in the executive. During the G. W. Bush presidency of 2000–04 and after he was re-elected for a second term as the 'war president', debate arose over whether a new 'imperial presidency' was developing, with the expansion of unchecked presidential authority.

In particular, the notion developed of a 'unitary executive', where it was asserted that the original intent of the Founding Fathers had been to create a strong executive — this, in effect, justifying the increase in executive power.

Certainly Congress was more docile, and the Supreme Court between 2001 and 2004 refrained from entering the political thicket. This was helped by Republican control of Congress from 2000 to 2006, with a more ideologically cohesive, conservative Republican party controlling the committees and the legislative process and deferring to President Bush's wishes and demands concerning national security. This was evidenced in:

- the passage of the Patriot Act, with its controversial authority for a 'security state' through domestic surveillance and wire-tapping, widely thought to be unconstitutional as against personal freedoms and privacy
- Guantánamo Bay and the setting up of military commissions to try 'enemy combatant' cases, ignoring habeas corpus and due process
- the setting up of the Homeland Security Department
- the resolution to go to war with Iraq (passed by 296 votes to 133 in the House and by 77 to 23 in the Senate), with the costs of war funded
- the increasing use of executive orders and claims of executive privilege

Bush also added 'signing statements' to bills before he signed them into law, showing his disapproval of some parts and indicating how he thought they should be applied. In effect this was a line-item veto in all but name and it was argued that the president was straying too far into legislative action, which was not part of his constitutional power.

So a swinging of the pendulum back towards executive-branch exercise of power between 2001and 2006 was accompanied by a weakness in congressional oversight.

However, Republican losses in the 2006 mid-term elections, with Congress now in the control of Democrats ready to flex their political muscles, left Bush a lame-duck president for his last 2 years of office. His approval ratings were below 30% for much of this time, because of the increasingly unpopular wars in Iraq and Afghanistan and the developing economic crisis in 2008.

President Obama

The election of President Obama in 2008, with strong Democrat majorities in both houses of Congress, has changed the situation again. In the midst of a severe economic crisis, the new president, a former lecturer in constitutional law, promised a bipartisan, pragmatic approach to the presidential–congressional relationship and the challenges that engulfed America in 2008.

It is likely that there will be little use of the veto or signing statements and no talk of a unitary executive, as a probable rebalancing of executive–congressional power unfolds in the future.

The new president, a Washington insider, took office with:
- a huge personal mandate
- high approval ratings
- political and personal charisma and the power to persuade

but also with:

- continuing Iraq and Afghanistan wars and an unstable world
- economic depression, a banking crisis and high and rising unemployment
- criticism from the right for going too far to the left and from the left for not going far enough
- the lack of a filibuster-proof Senate of 60 Democrat votes (see p. 31)

Presidential resources

The institutions of the modern presidency

Huge resources are needed to carry out the role of the modern presidency in the world's biggest government. All executive power may be vested in one president but the reality today is that of a vast 'institutional presidency' within a vast executive branch of government. With the huge growth of government activity since 1787, various institutions have developed to help the president fulfil his constitutional roles and much of what is done in the president's name is done by other people. However, the president is the only elected member (apart from the vice-president) with responsibility for all decisions taken. As Truman said when he was president, 'the buck stops here'.

The role of the vice-president

Although the vice-president 'balances the ticket' in a presidential election, the office of vice-president is traditionally perceived to be lacking significance, with no constitutional role apart from presiding over the Senate and brokering a tied vote. However, the office has changed somewhat in recent years: Dick Cheney was believed to be the power behind the throne in the George W. Bush presidency and the most powerful vice-president in US history, and Al Gore was in charge of the 'reinventing government' initiative during the Clinton presidency. A 'heartbeat away from the presidency', the main constitutional significance of the office is that the vice-president will become president if the incumbent president dies in office.

The presidential cabinet

The US cabinet has no constitutional status and is not mentioned in the Constitution other than as a possible body of advisers the president *may* take advice from. According to one scholar, Richard Fenno, any role it has is 'institutionalised by usage alone'. The US cabinet operates, therefore, by convention; *all* executive power is vested in the president. The USA has a singular executive, with no collective decision taking or collective responsibility. This is in contrast to a plural executive, such as the UK's cabinet government.

The cabinet contains the heads of the federal government departments; the director of the Office of Management and Budget and the vice-president also attend. The president does not need to call any cabinet meetings and their use has been variable according to the wishes of the president and the circumstances of the time. Nor does he have to take their advice — he has alternative sources of advice in the Executive Office (see below).

What are the functions of the cabinet?

Cabinet members are responsible to the president for the federal departments that they head. As such they:

- implement the president's agenda in their specialist area
- appear before the powerful congressional committees to represent the president's wishes and plead for funding and support for the president's policies
- attend meetings with the president, if and when required, to give advice. Often these are bilateral meetings to advise rather than full cabinet ones to discuss. Why would the Secretary of State want or need to know what is going on in the Agriculture Department?
- assist the president when full cabinet meetings are called to coordinate policy between the various federal departments involved in US government

How is the cabinet selected?

When presidents win office they select their cabinet secretaries during the transition period between November and January when the 'spoils of office' are distributed. There is no shadow cabinet in the USA and the president cannot select his cabinet from Congress because of the separation of powers. If members of Congress accept a cabinet post they must resign their congressional seats.

Otherwise cabinet members can come from anywhere — academia or business, for example — and the president has a free hand in their selection. Generally, the president-elect will be influenced by the following factors in his choices:

- They will be policy specialists, not generalists (as in the UK), chosen for their expertise and ability to head the specific federal department. They may not be politically experienced but will need some political skills to carry out their role.
- They have to be confirmed by the Senate after hearings.
- The president may wish to construct a cabinet which 'looks like America', providing some ethnic, gender or geographical balance and diversity, or, like Obama, a 'cabinet of rivals' to inspire debate.
- Generally, presidents choose political allies to provide partisan support, but they can be from a different party to the president to demonstrate bipartisanship.

How important is the cabinet to the president?

The power of the cabinet is not fixed and unchanging. It depends on variables such as the personalities involved or the governing style of the president. There may be a relatively inexperienced Washington-outsider president, willing to delegate to strong and experienced cabinet members, as in the case of President George W. Bush with Dick Cheney and Condoleezza Rice, for example, with the president relying on them for policy advice. Or there may be a strong Washington-insider president like Kennedy, who rarely called a cabinet meeting.

There is no set pattern, and evidence can be found from the study of different presidents and the variable use of their cabinets and the circumstances and issues dominating at the time (war or peace, recession or economic boom).

It is often said that presidents do not trust their cabinet secretaries' close links and loyalty to the federal department that they head and its permanent bureaucracy, nor their strong links with congressional committees and special interest lobbies because of their shared interests and close relationships. It is feared that they 'go native' or are captured in the so-called iron triangles, where policies are made and executed to the benefit of all parts of the triangle. Presidents are also aware of 'clientelism', where close links develop between the agencies and those they are supposed to be regulating (known as 'agency capture'). The presidential policy agenda is lost sight of in the process, with the president unable to exercise control.

This is why presidents turn to their political 'cronies' and advisers in EXOP.

The Executive Office of the President (EXOP)

EXOP is an umbrella term covering the various offices that developed after the observation of the 1937 Brownlow Committee, as the role of the presidency grew, that 'the President needs help'. EXOP has been described as the principal instrument of presidential government and as the president's personal bureaucracy. Working under the direct control of the president (unlike the cabinet members who may have divided loyalties), EXOP is used to direct and control the executive branch of government. New parts have been added to EXOP since its creation in 1939, as the domestic and foreign policy demands on the president have increased.

Today EXOP includes the following:

The White House Office (WHO)

Often described as the 'invisible presidency', the WHO is made up of the president's closest aides. The key figure is the chief of staff, but the office also includes the president's speechwriters, congressional liaison team and press officers. The function of the WHO is to:
- act as gatekeeper, controlling access to the president (Nixon's key aides were nicknamed the 'Berlin Wall' for their success in this task)
- decide policy strategy and priorities for the president
- manage the news
- build support for the president's proposals in Congress

The National Security Council (NSC)

Headed by the national security adviser, the NSC advises the president on domestic, foreign and military matters relating to national security. It competes for power and the 'ear of the president' with the State Department and the Defense Department; this can lead to conflicts within US foreign policy, for example over the conduct of the war with Iraq.

The Office of Management and Budget (OMB)

The OMB constructs the federal budget, thus coordinating the legislative priorities and spending plans of the federal government departments and agencies. The OMB may provide different advice to the president from that given by the treasury secretary or the Council of Economic Advisers, which is also in EXOP.

Why is EXOP so important to the president?

The president relies on the advice and expertise of EXOP as an alternative to that coming from the cabinet secretaries, who may have conflicting interests (see p. 50). In contrast, the president trusts his advisers in EXOP, who are loyal only to him and his needs and wishes, and who follow his agenda.

What criticisms are made of EXOP?

- The president can become isolated, remote and overprotected from the realities of life outside the Oval Office, listening only to his 'political cronies', who have often come with him into the West Wing from his home state, and taking advice only from them. Examples include Karl Rove, Bush's close adviser, and David Axelrod for Obama.
- EXOP is unelected and unaccountable despite its huge power and influence, with few of its members subject to Senate confirmation or to congressional oversight as cabinet members are.
- 'Policy drift' occurs, with disputes between the cabinet secretaries and their EXOP counterparts, leaving the president perhaps caught between the conflicting advice.

The role of the federal bureaucracy

The federal bureaucracy consists of the officials in the federal government departments, executive agencies and regulatory commissions, who are employed by the state to advise on and carry out the policies of the political executive. All these organisations are created and funded by Congress. A bureaucracy is indispensable to the operation of modern government to run the core functions of the state. However, it lacks the legitimacy that comes from election and takes no electoral responsibility for the decisions that are made. It is described as the state's engine room, as it drives everything in government.

In the USA, the 15 federal government departments are headed by cabinet secretaries but staffed by hierarchically organised federal bureaucrats, most of whom are permanent. However, some appointments are political (and therefore temporary) appointments made by an incoming president.

It is argued that permanent status gives bureaucrats detailed policy knowledge and expertise. This, it is argued, allows them to influence policy initiation through their advice on options, and also have control over policy implementation once laws have been passed by Congress and signed by the president. They are therefore in a good position to influence the working of public policy and are accountable only to their political heads, the cabinet secretaries, and, through them, to the president.

In theory, the federal bureaucracy works under the direction of the president, but in practice it is difficult, if not impossible, for a president to 'command and control' and make the bureaucracy do what he wants it to do. As Truman said, 'I thought I was the President but when it comes to these bureaucracies I can't make 'em do a damn thing.' Other presidents have expressed similar sentiments about the relationships between cabinet secretaries, congressional committees, interest groups and federal bureaucrats who have strong views on American public policy and how it should be made and carried out. All presidents, at some stage in their presidency, express reservations about the bureaucracy and their policy views, which become entrenched and hard to change.

Comparisons with the UK executive

The UK executive works under an uncodified constitution, with constitutional conventions largely determining its operation.

The prime minister

- The office is based on convention, so the powers of the office can be stretched.
- The prime minister is not elected with his or her own mandate but is simply the majority party leader.
- As majority leader, the prime minister exercises the powers of the royal prerogative, such as patronage or dissolution powers.
- Although the prime minister has power over the cabinet, he or she is *primus inter pares* — first among equals — within it. Different prime ministers run their cabinets in different ways according to their style of government (for example, more dominant or more collegial).
- The prime minister's appointments are not checked or rejected by the legislature.
- The prime minister can be removed by internal party procedures or by a successful vote of no confidence in the Commons; the latter removes the whole government from office.
- The prime minister has nothing remotely equivalent to the resources provided to the US president by EXOP. However, more resources are being developed to serve the prime minister alone, for example the Prime Minister's Office.
- The prime minister does not 'tread the world stage' with global responsibilities.
- There are arguments that the office has become 'presidentialised', but this may be to do with the personal governing styles of certain 'strong' prime ministers.

The UK cabinet

- Constitutionally, by convention, the UK has cabinet government.

- It is a plural executive, with collective decision making and collective responsibility (CCR) to the House of Commons for all decisions made.
- Members of the cabinet have individual responsibility (IMR) for running their department and must answer to the House of Commons for this.
- They are generalists, not specialists, as cabinet reshuffles take place frequently.
- Cabinet members are drawn from the legislature, usually elected MPs but occasionally Lords, and are political figures in their own right.
- The cabinet meets weekly under the direction of the prime minister, who decides the composition of cabinet, the cabinet agenda and so on.
- Lack of cabinet support may lead to the prime minister's downfall, as in 1990 with Margaret Thatcher.

The UK civil service

- The civil service is permanent, neutral and selected by merit. There are no political appointments of civil servants or 'spoils of office' (although the number of ministerial special advisers is growing).
- The civil service is anonymous. It works under the direction and control of elected ministers, who have individual responsibility.
- There may be strong departmental views as to what is best in terms of policy but there are no iron triangles or clientelism — although strong insider groups may have access.
- It is sometimes argued that a 'rule by officials' lies behind a façade of representation and accountability. The problem of organisation and control of bureaucratic power is one that no political system finds easy to solve.

The judicial branch of government: the Supreme Court

The judicial power of the Supreme Court, the third branch of US government, comes from Article 3 of the Constitution. The Supreme Court was to be the guardian of the sovereign, entrenched document, containing the USA's fundamental law and core values.

The court today plays a very different role from that envisaged in 1787 and debate revolves round whether it can be seen as a political as well as a judicial institution, with the justices simply 'politicians in robes sitting on a bench'.

Why is the Supreme Court so important in the US system of government?

- The Supreme Court has the power of constitutional interpretation of the vague language of the document and its amendments.
- The Supreme Court resolves the conflicts that arise over the constitutional workings of the branches and layers of American government, and over the protection of rights entrenched in the Bill of Rights.
- By convention, the Supreme Court has the power of judicial review, which it 'discovered' in the **Marbury v Madison** case of 1803 when it first declared an Act unconstitutional.

What is judicial review?

The power of judicial review allows the Supreme Court to declare laws or parts of laws passed by Congress and the president to be incompatible with the Constitution and therefore void. An example would be the use of the line-item veto struck down by the court in *Clinton* v *City of New York* in 1998. The first time the court declared a state law unconstitutional was in the *Fletcher* v *Peck* case in 1810. Presidential actions can also be declared unconstitutional, as, for example, Nixon's claim of executive privilege over the Watergate tapes in 1973.

This power of judicial review was *not* in the Constitution itself. The *Marbury* v *Madison* (1803) judgement effectively determined that the Constitution is superior to the laws passed by Congress, thereby increasing the interpretational power of the Supreme Court. The court's power of judicial review over presidential, congressional and state actions, determining their constitutionality, is the *main* reason why the Supreme Court is often described as a political as well as a judicial institution.

A brief history of the Supreme Court

Until 1865, cases coming before the court involved issues relating to federal–state relations and slavery. For example, the *Dred Scott* v *Sandford* case in 1857 concluded that slavery was constitutional. From the 1870s to the 1940s, cases related more to state regulation of the economy. With economic issues largely settled, the emphasis then shifted to civil liberties and civil rights cases, such as those determined by the Warren and Burger courts in the mid-twentieth century. These were both 'judicially activist' courts, whereas the Rehnquist Court (1986–2005) was a court of more 'judicial restraint'. (We return to these differences in more detail in the section 'Judicial philosophy' below.) The current court is the Roberts Court.

How are Supreme Court justices appointed?

The 'political' role of the court is reinforced by the process of appointing justices, which is arguably influenced more by political than judicial factors. The president nominates, but his nomination has to be confirmed by the Senate with a simple majority. This two-stage process can be especially problematic when there is divided government, with one party controlling the White House and another with a majority in the Senate, as political acceptability is the key to both nomination and confirmation:

- Presidents use their power of nomination to reinforce their political position and to leave a legacy on the Supreme Court. Presidents have a maximum of 8 years in office, whereas their Supreme Court nominee(s) can be on the court for decades.
- Presidents can use their power of nomination to gain support from key groups, for example Lyndon Johnson's appointment in 1967 of the first black justice, Thurgood Marshall, and Reagan's 1981 appointment of the first female justice, Sandra Day O'Connor.
- Republican presidents nominate 'conservative' justices with a philosophy of judicial restraint and 'strict constructionism'. Democrat presidents nominate 'liberal' justices with a philosophy of judicial activism and 'loose constructionism'. (These terms are covered in more detail below under 'Judicial philosophy'.)
- The appointment process is particularly important when 'swing justices' retire or die and have to be replaced. Their departure may alter the balance of the Supreme Court and the dominant judicial philosophy, thus affecting the judgements likely to be made. This was the case when Justice Sandra Day O'Connor retired in 2005.

Several judicial appointments have been particularly controversial:

- In 1987, the Senate rejected Reagan's nominee, Robert Bork. Although a distinguished legal scholar, Bork's highly conservative judicial views were unacceptable to the Democrat-controlled Senate. By rejecting the nomination, the Senate denied Reagan his wish to shift the court towards a more conservative judicial philosophy.
- George Bush's nominee in 1991, the black but highly conservative Clarence Thomas, scraped through the Senate Judiciary Committee hearings after the lowest American Bar Association rating ever for a potential justice and was only just confirmed by the whole Senate on a vote of 52 to 48.
- G. W. Bush's initial nomination of his White House counsel, Harriet Miers, to replace Rehnquist in 2005 had to be withdrawn after it became clear that her lack of judicial experience meant confirmation was unlikely, even from a Republican-controlled Senate.

The importance of the president's powers of appointment can, however, be over-estimated:

- The president can appoint *only* when a vacancy arises, as when a justice has died or retired. Some presidents are fortunate and get to appoint several justices: Reagan appointed three; George Bush and George W. Bush appointed two each; and Clinton also appointed two. Carter, in contrast, appointed none in his 4 years as president.
- The president cannot remove justices or influence their judgements once they are on the court.
- He has no guarantees that justices will do what he wants, as their future decisions are unpredictable. Most presidents express regrets about their choices; Eisenhower referred to his selection of fellow conservative Earl Warren as chief justice as 'the biggest damn fool mistake I ever made' when Warren went on to lead the most activist court in US history.
- The political considerations in the appointment process may be less than is generally suspected. Justices are not loyal to any administration. They are independent, and their judicial decisions are influenced by legal and constitutional, not political, factors.
- The current Supreme Court has six Republican-nominated justices and only three Democrat ones, but it is not a predictable court and, like Warren, many justices change when they are on the court.

Judicial independence

This is the principle that there should be a strict separation between the judiciary and the other branches of government, and is fundamental to the idea of the rule of law. Judges operate free from any political control over their behaviour. The key to judicial independence is security of tenure, with judges holding office for life, on condition of 'good behaviour'. They cannot be removed for political reasons or for the judgements they make; they can be removed only through successful impeachment by the House and Senate for reasons of personal conduct.

Judicial philosophy

To understand the Supreme Court it is important to be aware of different judicial philosophies leading to different views on the interpretation of the Constitution by justices. Courts can be judicially active or judicially restrained, depending on the use of their power of judicial review. The Warren and Burger courts, as mentioned above, were judicially activist. The Rehnquist Court was more judicially restrained. The current court, the Roberts Court, as yet shows no clear discernible trends in its judicial decisions.

What is judicial activism?

Judicially active justices and courts are those that adhere to 'loose constructionism'. This means that they interpret the words of the Constitution in the light of modern conditions and current reality, reading into the words of the Constitution their views of what is best for the country at the present time.

A judicially active court of loose construction, such as the Warren Court, would 'innovate' through landmark rulings: for example, extending civil liberties and rights and generally favouring the expansion of federal power.

The Warren Court 1953–69

This court, led by Chief Justice Earl Warren, was a liberal, activist, loose construc-tionist court whose numerous landmark decisions were alleged to have brought about a constitutional revolution. The Warren Court took the initiative in several areas where the elected branches of government, president and Congress, were either unable or unwilling to act. The court had a huge impact on American life through many of its judicial decisions, in particular the following:

- ***Brown* v *Board of Education of Topeka, Kansas* (1954).** The court ruled (9–0) that the 'separate but equal' doctrine established in the *Plessy* v *Ferguson* case in 1896 was unconstitutional as it denied the 'equal protection of the laws' clause of the Fourteenth Amendment. This case began the dismantling of racial segre-gation in the USA and galvanised the Civil Rights Movement.
- ***Miranda* v *Arizona* (1966).** This judgement led to 'Miranda rights', based on the Fifth Amendment, giving additional rights to criminal suspects when arrested.

The judgements of the Warren Court became a factor in the 1968 presidential election, when Nixon pledged to put on to the court 'law and order' judges who would 'inter-pret the Constitution and not impose their own beliefs' or 'legislate from the bench'. G. W. Bush made similar comments in 2005.

The question was, and still is, were the justices behaving like politicians, and was the court behaving like a legislature? Regardless of the rightness of the justices' decisions, was the court the right institution to take them?

The Burger Court 1969–86

This court, led by Chief Justice Warren Burger, was predicted to be more judicially restrained than the Warren Court but was more activist than expected, and many of its judgements were, and continue to be, controversial:

- ***Roe* v *Wade* (1973).** Using the shadows or 'penumbras' of the Constitution, the court ruled (7–2) that abortion *was* constitutional and part of a woman's implied right to privacy. This decision, in effect, brought about the pro-choice and pro-life movements that are so active in American political life today. The religious right in particular has lobbied for a constitutional amendment to overturn *Roe* v *Wade*, as the Supreme Court has always upheld its 1973 judgement.

- *Swann* v *Charlotte-Mecklenburg Board of Education* **(1971).** The court made a controversial decision allowing bussing to achieve more racial balance in schools under the 'equal protection' clause of the Fourteenth Amendment.

The Warren and Burger courts are good examples of the enormous political and social effects of Supreme Court judgements, as opposed to the decisions made by the president and Congress. Both courts alienated American conservatives and provoked a backlash against what was seen as judicial tyranny and the quasi-legislative power of the Supreme Court. There was even an 'Impeach Earl Warren' movement in the southern states!

What is judicial restraint?

Judicially restrained justices and courts are those that follow a judicial philosophy of 'strict constructionism' and 'original intent'. This means that they interpret the Constitution more literally and make their judgements based on the words of the original document as written by the Founding Fathers and their intentions at the time. This involves a much narrower interpretation of the Constitution. Generally speaking, a court of judicial restraint avoids innovation and controversial landmark rulings, favours states' rights and follows precedent (*stare decisis*). It is said that such courts do not wish to enter the political thicket on controversial cases, deferring to the elected and responsible branches of government.

The Rehnquist Court 1986–2005

This court, headed by Rehnquist (appointed chief justice by Reagan), was a more restrained court compared to the previous courts. However, it was not easily classifiable and was often divided in its judgements between four 'conservative' justices (Rehnquist, Scalia, Thomas and Kennedy) and four 'liberal' justices (Souter, Breyer, Stevens and Ginsberg). The crucial member of this court was Sandra Day O'Connor, as she was the deciding swing justice on many of the 5–4 knife-edge decisions. These included judgements on abortion, and on affirmative action and racial quotas, such as *Grutter* v *Bollinger* in 2003. A significant 5–4 case, decided in 2000, was *Bush* v *Gore*, which ruled that the Florida recount of ballots after the close election of that year was unconstitutional under the 'equal protection' clause of the Fourteenth Amendment. This case was highly politically charged; in effect, the judgement by the court, seven of whose members had been appointed by Republicans, including two by his father, handed the election to George W. Bush.

The Roberts Court from 2005

The death of Chief Justice Rehnquist and the retirement of Sandra Day O'Connor gave Bush the opportunity to reshape the Supreme Court and leave a conservative legacy on it. He expressed admiration for the two strictest constructionists on the court — Scalia and Thomas — and, in 2005, nominated John Roberts to replace Rehnquist (a conservative replacing a conservative, so no change there). Roberts was confirmed by a 78–22 vote in the Senate showing some controversy (Senator Obama voted against the nomination). Roberts promised 'not to legislate from the bench' in his Senate hearings.

The key change was the appointment of Alito, who had a conservative record as a judge on litmus-test issues like abortion, to replace the swing justice O'Connor. Again the Senate confirmation was not easy, with the 58–42 vote showing much (Democrat) opposition.

These appointments, changing the balance of the court, may or may not prove to be Bush's judicial legacy to the USA. Supreme Court justices are *not* predictable in their judicial behaviour, however, and there is a new swing justice, Kennedy (a Reagan appointee), who has been found on the majority side of 5–4 votes in recent cases brought before the still frequently divided court.

- One controversial case, decided in 2006, was **Hamdan v Rumsfeld**. The court made a landmark ruling (5–3, with Roberts not participating) that the president had exceeded his constitutional powers as commander-in-chief by setting up military commissions detaining in Guantánamo Bay. Bush had argued that this was justified in the war on terror. The court ruled that the 'enemy combatants' (al-Qaida suspects) were entitled to due process of law, thus defending civil liberties in the face of an overpowerful executive and, in effect, reining in an 'imperial presidency' by what some now call the 'imperial judiciary'.
- **Gonzales v Carhart (2007)** was passed by a 5–4 majority (with Kennedy as the swing justice). The ruling upheld the constitutionality of the law passed by Congress in 2003 banning partial-birth abortions, which some argue is chipping away at the Roe rights. This case may be evidence of the difference that a change in justice can bring about (a similar law had previously been struck down) and a more rightward shift by the court.

Whether the Supreme Court would have been different if Kerry had won the 2004 election is something we can only speculate about, but the likely answer is 'yes', as the new 5–4 decisions are beginning to show.

The protection of rights by the Supreme Court

The 'inalienable rights' of US citizens are entrenched in the first ten amendments, the Bill of Rights, and are protected by the Supreme Court, using its powers of constitutional interpretation and judicial review. It is important to note that the court often has to balance competing rights in its judgements; there are no absolute rights.

Generally speaking, it is activist courts of loose construction that extend rights through their landmark rulings.

Rights of minorities

***Grutter* v *Bollinger* (2003)** said racial profiling was constitutional for university admissions if it was 'individualised' and not done by quotas or preferential treatment.

Religion

***Engel* v *Vitale* (1962)** upheld the First Amendment's guarantee of freedom of religion and denial of an establishment of religion. It was the Founding Fathers' wish for a separation of church and state, so there could be no prayers (or religious activity) in schools or public places.

Freedom of speech

Texas* v *Johnson* (1989)** struck down a state law banning desecration of the flag as infringing the First Amendment freedom of expression provisions. When Congress passed a law banning flag desecration, that too was struck down in ***United States* v *Eichman in 1990 and declared unconstitutional.

The right to bear arms

In June 2008 the Supreme Court, in ***District of Columbia* v *Heller***, struck down (5–4) a Washington DC gun law banning hand-guns as incompatible with the Second Amendment. Thus it upheld an individual's constitutional right to bear arms. This was the first pronouncement on the Second Amendment in the entire history of the Supreme Court.

However, as we saw in the earlier section on the Constitution, rights in the USA have not always been fully protected by the Constitution and the Bill of Rights or by its interpreters in the Supreme Court. This is particularly the case if the Supreme Court is judicially restrained and following principles of strict construction and original intent.

What are the main constraints on the power of the Supreme Court?

There is little doubt that the Supreme Court's powers of constitutional interpretation and judicial review give it enormous power in the US system of constitutional government and many of its landmark cases have been politically controversial. However, the court is *not* all-powerful and it operates under several constraints. These are as follows:

- It is a reactive court and only rules on cases that are appealed to it. It does not initiate its own cases.
- Congress has power to alter the number of justices on the court. This was threatened when the court was obstructive to parts of the New Deal and Roosevelt threatened his 'court-packing' plan to overcome this obstruction. The court backed

down and the numbers on the court have not been changed since the 1869 Judiciary Act.

- Supreme Court interpretation of the Constitution can be overturned by constitutional amendment, as in 1913 when the Sixteenth Amendment allowed a federal income tax to be levied, thus overcoming the Supreme Court's ruling that this was unconstitutional. This has been suggested as a way of dealing with issues such as abortion or flag burning, where the court's decisions have angered groups, who then lobby for an amendment. If one were passed, the Supreme Court would have to interpret the new amendment — it could not overturn it. However, although often threatened, this eventuality is unlikely to occur, as it would be difficult to gather the required support in Congress and the states.
- The court can exercise judicial *self*-restraint by refusing to hear cases appealed to it. An example is the Schiavo 'right to die' case in 2005. Decisions to ignore cases indicate that the court is deferring to the elected branches of government and refusing to enter the political thicket or go against prevailing public opinion on particular issues.
- The court lacks the power to enforce its decisions, and has to rely on both political and public acceptance that its decision was the 'right' one. In 1954 the court was unable to enforce its decision in the *Brown* v *Board of Education* case to de-segregate 'with all deliberate speed'. The southern states refused to de-segregate, claiming that states' rights allowed them not to. In 1957 President Eisenhower famously had to send federal troops into Little Rock, Arkansas, to enforce de-segregation of the high school, and, 10 years after Brown, the southern states were still not fully de-segregated. The Civil Rights Act finally ended segregation by federal law in 1964.
- Some Supreme Court decisions are ignored, such as the continuation of religious activity in some public areas despite the court's ruling in *Engel* v *Vitale*.

The Supreme Court: a 'political' or 'judicial' body?

This has always been one of the central debates in American government and there are no right or wrong answers to it. Some commentators have used terms such as 'judicial policy making' and 'quasi-legislative judicial authority' to show the contradictions. It is not an easy question to answer because the role of the Supreme Court is paradoxical.

A political body?

On the one hand, these nine persons, appointed for life, meet behind closed doors to make decisions, often with a narrow margin of 5–4, on the major political issues affecting the American people, with no accountability to anyone for those decisions. They will deliberate and make rulings on issues such as:

- Is abortion constitutional?
- Can hand-guns be banned?
- What are the limits on free speech?
- Is affirmative action the right way to solve deep-seated problems of racial discrimination?
- Can suspected terrorists be held at Guantánamo Bay without trial?
- Is the death penalty 'cruel and unusual' punishment?

They are also able, through the power of judicial review, to strike down decisions made by the democratically elected representatives of the people in the White House, Congress and the states.

Whereas, in the USA, it is the Supreme Court that decides controversial political questions like those listed above, in other countries, such as the UK, those same issues would be decided by elected and accountable politicians and regarded as political rather than judicial questions. In this sense, the Supreme Court is not and cannot be 'above politics'. Its powers of constitutional interpretation of the codified document and its entrenched rights and of judicial review of state and congressional legislation and presidential actions inevitably bring it into the political arena and give it a political role.

A judicial body?

On the other hand, the Supreme Court is a judicial institution and follows judicial procedures. The nine members are justices who believe it their duty to interpret the words of the sovereign constitution in order to ascertain its meaning. They are not politicians representing electorates. They have used their powers selectively and sparingly over the 220 years of the court's existence.

The central paradox

Finally, it is said that the central paradox of the USA, which takes so much pride in its elective democracy, is the existence of the unelected Supreme Court and its unchecked power to decide crucial questions. The court provides constitutional solutions to what elsewhere would be seen as political problems to be decided politically and not judicially. A key question, therefore, is 'Who guards the guardians?'

Comparisons with the UK judiciary

- In the UK, there is no entrenched codified constitution needing judicial interpretation.
- Parliamentary sovereignty means there can be no challenge to laws passed by

Parliament. There is no 'higher law' and nothing passed by Parliament can be unconstitutional.

- The judiciary can hear *ultra vires* (beyond the power) cases testing whether ministers have acted outside the powers granted to them by parliamentary statute making their actions 'unlawful'.
- The judiciary can issue 'declarations of incompatibility' if they think that parliamentary legislation contravenes the provisions of the 1998 Human Rights Act. Parliament does not have to act on this, however, as that would contradict the sovereignty of Parliament.
- The judiciary in the UK is therefore less powerful than its counterpart in the USA, with much weaker powers of judicial review.
- Rights are less protected in the UK because they are not entrenched (and cannot be because of parliamentary sovereignty). Government may also 'derogate' from the provisions of the Human Rights Act if it wishes to pass legislation that will clash with the rights contained in the European Convention of Human Rights.

Judicial appointment

- Judicial appointments used to be made by the prime minister after advice from the Lord Chancellor. There were criticisms of 'cronyism' and secrecy inherent in these 'soundings'.
- There is no confirmation process in Parliament.
- The 2005 Constitutional Reform Act abolished the office of Lord Chancellor and a new independent Judicial Appointments Commission (JAC) was established to appoint judges.
- In 2010, the 12 Law Lords will move from the House of Lords to a new 'Supreme Court', strengthening the separation of powers, although they will still operate under parliamentary sovereignty.

Growing judicial activism in the UK

Although an uncodified constitution and parliamentary sovereignty give the UK judiciary little scope for any influence, the judiciary has become more willing to challenge the executive:

- There has been an increase in judicial review and in the number of *ultra vires* cases.
- There have been clashes between the judiciary and ministers, for example on detention without trial.
- A 'rights culture' has developed since the implementation of the Human Rights Act, although this offers nowhere near the protection found in the USA's entrenched Bill of Rights. The 'declarations of incompatibility' bring judges further into the political arena.
- UK membership of the EU has extended the role of the courts, particularly since the Factortame case, which established the supremacy of EU law in the event of a clash with UK law.

Questions
&
Answers

This section looks at answers to examination questions on Unit 4A, and follows the four areas identified in the specification: the constitutional framework of US government, and the legislative, executive and judicial branches.

The examination paper gives a two-part 40-mark question, divided into part (a), worth 10 marks (to be done in around 10 minutes), and part (b), worth 30 marks (to be done in around 35 minutes), for each of these four areas. Candidates must choose two questions out of the four to answer. The time available is 90 minutes.

On the following pages, each question is accompanied by two answers written under timed conditions. One is of A-grade standard and the other of C-grade standard. None of the answers should be regarded as a perfect response. Each one simply represents a way of approaching the actual question set, and is followed by an indication of the grade it is likely to achieve and why.

After each of the questions, there is a section (indicated by the symbol ℮) identifying the focus of the question and what is expected in the answer. Each answer is followed by an examiner's comment, also indicated by the symbol ℮: this section comments on the approach of the answer and explains some of the reasons why it has achieved the grade indicated or how a higher mark could have been gained. If you read these sections carefully, you will get an idea of how to improve your marks in the examination for both parts of the question. It will also help you become more familiar with the assessment objectives.

It would be good practice to attempt your own answers before looking at the student answers and the comments made, so that you can compare and make any adjustments likely to increase your mark.

Note that the answers given here are not model answers that can be reproduced in an examination. Most examination questions are worded differently, even when they are in the same specification area, and it is possible to achieve exactly the same grade for a question in different ways, by scoring on the assessment objectives with different strengths, weaknesses, evidence and examples. At A2, remember the importance of analysis and evaluation (AO2) as well as knowledge and description (AO1), especially if you are to gain higher marks. You may also be rewarded for making connections with earlier AS studies, if they are appropriate and relevant, as this demonstrates synoptic understanding of political topics.

Question

The constitutional framework of US government

(a) Explain how citizens' rights are protected by the Constitution in the USA.

(10 marks)

> ✑ This question calls for an explanation of the entrenched Bill of Rights, the first ten amendments to the Constitution, as well as other constitutional amendments such as the Fourteenth, guaranteeing the 'equal protection of the laws', and the protection these give to the rights of American citizens. It also expects you to show knowledge of the role of the Supreme Court in protecting citizens' rights and to include in your answer at least one or two examples of specific guaranteed constitutional rights. For the very highest marks, you could question how effective these protections actually are in modern conditions, especially since 9/11 and the war on terror.

■ ■ ■

A-grade answer

In the USA, the first ten amendments to the Constitution, known as the Bill of Rights, lay out the rights of the American people as citizens. This is what Madison argued for when the Constitution was written in 1787. The American people are very aware of their 'inalienable' rights, guaranteed under the Constitution, in the Bill of Rights, such as the First Amendment, guaranteeing personal freedoms, and later amendments which guarantee women and ethnic minorities the vote.

In the USA, citizens' rights are protected in the codified Constitution, which is entrenched and 'supreme law'. This entrenchment ensures that the Constitution is sovereign, and therefore rights are guaranteed in the Constitution and cannot be breached by government. Social policy from various governments has attempted to control gun crime but has faced opposition from groups such as the NRA, who refer to the Second Amendment, guaranteeing the right to bear arms. However, although rights are protected by the Supreme Court, it can give different interpretations over time, such as saying that 'separate but equal' was constitutional in the Plessy case in 1896 but then reversing this ruling in the 1954 Brown case saying that segregation was 'inherently unequal' and therefore against the 'equal protection' clause guaranteed in the Fourteenth Amendment. So the protection of rights can depend on the Supreme Court at the time and the cases it is willing to hear.

> ✑ This candidate's answer is knowledgeable (AO1) and well argued (AO2). Political vocabulary is good, for example the use of the terms 'inalienable' and 'entrenched', which are clearly understood and used in context. The reference to Madison suggests good contextual awareness. There are references to the First,

Second and Fourteenth amendments as evidence and the role of the Supreme Court is understood vis-à-vis the protection of rights. The last sentence could have been further developed with reference to modern-day debate concerning the impact of 9/11 on rights in the USA, but the rest of the answer is of such high quality in all three assessment objectives that it would achieve a high A grade anyway.

■ ■ ■

C-grade answer

Many would argue that a codified constitution is a far better safeguard of the rights of citizens than the uncodified constitution of the UK. Inspired by philosophers like John Locke, the Founding Fathers put sovereignty and liberty of the people at the very heart of the Constitution. In the USA the Constitution and its amendments are the supreme law of the land, which no institution may ignore. The president, the Congress and the state legislatures cannot act to infringe the Bill of Rights, which contains all the rights that an individual is entitled to and they are constitutionally guaranteed. Though whether this is reflected in reality is open to question.

Many now argue that the US Bill of Rights has not sufficiently protected citizens from the provisions of the Patriot Act passed in 2001 and the detention without trial seen in Guantánamo Bay. Also, the right to vote guaranteed to black Americans by the Constitution after the Civil War was ignored by the southern states with little enforcement of those guaranteed constitutional rights by the Supreme Court.

This candidate does challenge the effectiveness of the protections of the Bill of Rights in the last paragraph and this is worthy of AO2 credit. There is also knowledge of the Bill of Rights and the 'supreme law' of the USA and an impressive contextual reference to Locke. However, the first sentence is not explained, and the lack of specific examples of any of the guaranteed rights in the Bill of Rights or any other amendments is a serious omission. Also, there is no explanation of the role of the Supreme Court in protecting constitutional rights. These are the reasons why this basically good answer would reach a very high C grade but no higher.

■ ■ ■

(b) How accurate is it to describe the US Constitution as too rigid and difficult to change?
(30 marks)

Here you should recognise in the question the debate over how 'rigid' the codified US Constitution actually is. This is due partly to the intentionally difficult amendment process prescribed by the document itself. It is essential that you include discussion of the amendment procedure in your answer to show the intentions of the Founding Fathers, with examples of both change (with 17 amendments to choose from) and lack of change (the entrenched first ten amendments or any of the numerous failed amendments). These examples would be necessary to demonstrate both the flexibility and the rigidity of the Constitution. You will also need to argue that change, and therefore flexibility, can come about through Supreme Court interpretation, especially in 'activist' courts such as Warren. You should give examples of cases effectively bringing about constitutional change without any change to the document itself, showing the adaptability of the Constitution to social and political developments. To gain top marks, you will need to refer to the flexibility brought to the Constitution by developing conventions and practices to 'fill in the gaps' where the Constitution is silent.

■ ■ ■

A-grade answer

The USA has a written codified constitution and as a result it may be described as too rigid and difficult to change. The UK, by contrast, has an unwritten constitution in the sense that it is not contained in one single document so it lacks a formal Constitution but is made up of a variety of different sources along with long-standing traditions. This has led to some saying that it is too flexible and easy to change.

The US Constitution is a written codified document, which has survived for over 200 years and is the cornerstone of American democracy and part of what it is to 'be an American'. It was intended to be a collection of fundamental principles for the new nation state. If they are such fundamental principles then it could, and possibly should, be argued that the Constitution is rightfully entrenched and difficult to change. When the Founding Fathers drew up the Constitution they were keen to ensure that the process of amending it was relatively hard, in order to ensure political stability over the years and the longevity of the document. In the USA, constitutional law is above that of ordinary statute law where there is a conflict between the two. In the UK, constitutional law does not exist, as 'constitutional changes' are implemented in exactly the same manner as statute law, by a simple majority in the sovereign Parliament, such as the devolution of power to Scotland in 1998. However, any change in power in the USA would need a constitutional amendment.

In order to amend the US Constitution the Founding Fathers stated that Congress must either call a national convention at the request of two-thirds of the state legislatures or there must be a two-thirds supermajority in favour of an amendment in both houses of Congress. Indeed the former has never been used. For a proposal to be ratified the Founding Fathers stipulated that there should be another supermajority in three-quarters of the state legislatures for this amendment to be added to the Constitution.

The relatively inflexible nature of the US Constitution is revealed through the number of amendments that have been made. Since the Bill of Rights, which was the inclusion of ten inalienable rights to the Constitution, there have been only 17 amendments made. Indeed two of these cancel each other out, these being the Eighteenth and the Twenty-first, regarding the prohibition of alcohol.

While it could be argued that this is appropriate rigidity, some would argue that it prevents the USA from adapting to changes in national culture and situations. They cite the 'right to bear arms' as the principal example, highlighting the nation's failure to impose stricter gun laws. However, the nature of constitutional change in the USA requires that a majority of the people put pressure on Congress to implement necessary changes. The fact that this has not happened shows that the Constitution is fulfilling its role and preventing fundamental changes based on minority views, just as it was designed to do.

While the limited number of amendments presents the US Constitution as being highly inflexible, it has been kept up to date through judicial interpretation. The Founding Fathers granted the judiciary the power to interpret the document and this has allowed the rules of the Constitution to be kept up to date. It has been flexible in the sense that it can evolve along with the changes in society. In this role the judiciary has been willing to interpret the words in the light of modern conditions and ignore precedent.

To conclude, while it may be argued that the US Constitution is too rigid and diffi-cult to change it must be noted that this was the desire of the Founding Fathers, as they wanted to ensure long-term political stability for America. Furthermore, they set in place, using the judiciary, the ability for the Constitution to be flexible in terms of its interpretation, thus allowing it to remain up to date.

> 🖉 This very well written response (AO3) presents valid and convincing counter-arguments to the 'too rigid' description of the US Constitution, but also defends its rigidity well (AO2). There is a clear understanding of the nature of constitutional rules and why they are necessary to ordered government. The amendment process is competently covered and examples are given (AO1). The role of the Supreme Court in interpreting the Constitution, and therefore applying a new meaning to the words in it, is also highly relevant, although examples of specific cases and different kinds of courts would clarify the argument more and would gain higher marks. Nevertheless, this highly focused and structured answer has a solid conceptual understanding, never strays from the question, and also uses some relevant comparisons with the UK Constitution, so it fully deserves an A grade.

■ ■ ■

C-grade answer

A constitution is a framework of rules which says how a country or governmental system should be run. It can be codified or uncodified.

The US Constitution was created by the Founding Fathers in the 1700s. They created a document which would underpin America. Some argue that the Constitution is out of date and should be changed for modern society. The 'right to bear arms' is a controversial issue and is often debated after shootings such as those at Virginia Tech. So far this has not been changed as many citizens see this as their constitutional right.

To make an amendment to the Constitution, three-quarters of states need to agree. This process is lengthy and often unsuccessful. This is how the Founding Fathers wanted it to be.

However, it is also argued that the US Constitution is vague and therefore open to interpretation, as the Supreme Court does regularly. Depending on the nature of the court, the Constitution is interpreted in different ways. The 1953–69 Warren Court was loose constructionist and many controversial rulings were made, such as *Brown* v *Topeka Board of Education*. This key ruling stopped segregation in schools.

Amendments have been made to the Constitution. The Bill of Rights is fundamental to US government and lays down the rights of citizens. The US Constitution has evolved over time.

In the UK there is no formal document and Parliament is sovereign, laying down rules and practices. Any Acts passed by Parliament are to be followed. This shows it is easy to change the uncodified constitution by passing a law. Unlike the US Constitution, there is no room for interpretation or vagueness. The UK Constitution does evolve, however, which means it is not outdated to the extent of the US Constitution.

It is clear that on the surface the US Constitution may appear unchangeable but this is not the case. It is vague enough to allow interpretation by the courts. This in turn allows it to evolve and be applied to modern society. Although the amendment process is rigid, it prevents maverick laws being passed and the Constitution being overrun with amendments. It is, however, harder to change than the UK Constitution due to its codified form.

🖉 Although this answer is basically sound in its knowledge and analysis, there is vagueness around some of the arguments, and statements such as 'The US Constitution has evolved over time' are not developed with supporting evidence. In addition, the amendment process is not fully understood or explained and there are no examples of the passage of, or failure to pass, amendments. Similarly, the role of the Supreme Court in constitutional interpretation is understood but undeveloped. There is much assertion in the response but the candidate does not back it up with clear evidence: what is meant by 'codified'? What is a 'loose constructionist' court? What does the candidate mean by 'maverick laws'? However, the answer does keep a focus and introduces some comparative evidence from the UK. As a result, it would achieve a C grade.

uestion

The legislative branch of government: US Congress

(a) How important is party as an influence over congressional voting behaviour?

(10 marks)

💡 To answer this question you need to evaluate the varying influences that affect congressional voting while focusing on party as just one of these influences. You should explain why party is a relatively weak influence on members of Congress (perhaps compared to MPs in the UK Parliament) but also demonstrate knowledge that recent changes in Congress may have led to the greater significance of party voting than in the past, giving some explanation of this too. For higher marks, and to address the 'how important' part of the question, you will need to identify other factors influencing congressional voting, such as constituents or pressure groups.

■ ■ ■

A-grade answer

It is a generally held view that parties are much looser and thus hold less influence in the American Congress than they do in the UK Parliament and this does seem to be the case.

In the USA, parties aren't as clear-cut as in the UK and there are many reasons for this. One in particular is the fact that the USA is a huge and very diverse country. Thus it would be difficult for a party with a rigid ideology to claim support from all areas of the country. A classic example of this would be the southern democrats. During the 1950s and 60s, the southern democrats were at their most prominent and although they were members of the Democratic Party they were very right wing, e.g. anti civil rights, yet the Democratic Party is more liberal and to the left of the Republican Party. This lack of cohesion shows parties have little influence on Congressmen. Voting in Congress is more influenced by regional issues and the needs of members' particular states and districts. Congressmen 'pork-barrel' to 'bring home the bacon' to the 'folks back home' to help them gain re-election. Voting is also influenced by pressure groups, which may help to finance re-election campaigns, which the party does not do.

The lack of a promotion structure (as in the UK from back bench to front bench), because of the separation of powers, means that there is little that a party can offer its members. Also, Congressmen can't rely on their party to get them re-elected as elections occur through primaries in which individual personality and personal views are by far the most important factors in electoral success.

That said, the speaker of the House of Representatives and the majority party leaders have influence over committee membership, which holds a higher status in Congress. Also, perhaps the USA is set to change. In 1994 it saw the first Republican victory in the House and Senate for 40 years. To consolidate this, the speaker of the House, Newt Gingrich, used the 'Contract with America' to galvanise the Republicans and make them a more cohesive conservative party under his leadership. This led to higher levels of party voting than had been the case previously. The Democratic Party in Congress has also lost its deeply conservative southern wing, who were rare party voters, and as a result the Democratic Party also has more cohesion when voting on issues.

However, the parties in Congress lack the party cohesion and loyalty of the UK parliamentary parties, with their vigorous whipping system, party discipline and the 'carrots of ministerial office', which cannot be used in the Congress to keep party voting in line. In the UK, most voters vote for the party and its manifesto, not for the individual as in most US elections.

So, in conclusion, the party is simply one factor in influencing votes in Congress and is not necessarily the most important one.

📝 This answer is fully focused on the question from the start, shows excellent contextual understanding and develops several lines of analysis (AO2), showing why party may not be as strong a factor affecting voting as it is in the UK Parliament. There is excellent evidence relating to recent changes in party cohesion, such as the impact of the 1994 Contract with America and the loss of the Democratic Party's southern wing, showing the use of up-to-date examples. Other influences on voting are included and assessed, leading to a very high A grade for this impressive answer.

■ ■ ■

C-grade answer

Party can play an important role in influencing the actions of members of Congress, providing a loyalty which often affects the way they vote.

However, the primary influence on the way Congressmen vote is loyalty to their constituents and they vote in Congress to gain concessions for their constituency with the aim of 'bringing home the pork' via cross-party voting.

In the UK Parliament, MPs are primarily concerned with party loyalty and backbench rebellions are rare, with MPs often described as 'lobby fodder' for their parties because of the strong whip system and party discipline. At the extreme, de-selection can be threatened and career prospects damaged. By contrast, the 'bargaining process' that takes place in Congress on votes creates a far less adversarial system than in the UK and members of Congress from different parties often vote together on issues. In the USA, the separation of powers reduces the sense of party reliance and loyalty, as the president cannot offer jobs to members of Congress in return for their loyalty and support. The weak party system in Congress also means that there are no sanctions that can be used to persuade members of

Congress to vote with their parties. As a result they are not 'loyal' to their party in Congress and are not 'lobby fodder' for their parties.

This answer addresses the specific question and attempts to explain congressional voting behaviour, but it lacks specific evidence and developed examples of any of the other factors that affect the way a member of Congress votes. Although comparative references to the UK are good and would be rewarded, the answer does stray a little too far towards the UK system, thereby failing to use the available time to give more attention to congressional voting, with party as just one variable affecting this. More explanation as to why members of Congress have weak party ties, plus why they may have closer ties to the 'folks back home' and to interest groups, would lift this answer from a high C grade into a clear B grade.

■ ■ ■

(b) Critically evaluate the role and activities of congressional committees. (30 marks)

This question demands a critical evaluation, not simply a description, of the powerful congressional committees. You will need to cover their role within Congress vis-à-vis the executive branch of government and also show knowledge and understanding of how committees actually operate in Congress within the legislative and oversight processes. You will be expected to include examples of these roles and processes, along with examples of specific congressional committees in the House and Senate, such as Rules, Conference, Armed Services, Judiciary, Appropriations, and an indication of how their membership is decided. Knowledge of *why* the congressional committees are so powerful is essential to your response but you should also keep a clear focus on the criticisms made of their role and power within the separation of powers system and the resulting checks and balances. These could be the gridlock of the legislative process, or the failure of oversight due to iron triangles. You could legitimately refer to the much weaker parliamentary committees in the UK to demonstrate understanding gained from your AS studies.

■ ■ ■

A-grade response

Woodrow Wilson once said that the USA had 'government by the chairmen of the standing committees'. He was frustrated by the power of these committees and is one of a long line of people to criticise the influence they are able to exert over both legislation and the actions of the executive branch of government. All Senators and Congressmen sit on at least one committee and they are seen as a very important part of a politician's legislative and oversight duty. The standing committees are responsible for overseeing a particular area of government (such as agriculture or veterans' affairs) and the members of the committee are permanent (due to the incumbency effect in US politics, they often sit on that committee for a number of years), which means that they gain expert knowledge in the field that they operate in and are well placed to tackle the executive and to check and balance its power.

The president is detached from both the legislature and the law-making process, so he relies on his allies in Congress to push legislation through for him. However, it is the chairmen of the standing committees who have the final say over whether a piece of legislation is adopted by the committee for discussion. Only if it is adopted can it pass through the relevant legislative process in order to be made a law. The committee has the power to summon anyone to come and give evidence to it, and as its debates and activities are often televised it can gain a huge amount of media attention and, therefore, power. It is in these committees that politicians are said to forge their reputation and they pork-barrel here to gain amendments to legislation that will please their constituents (but not the president) and help their re-election. This is a criticised part of the committees' activities as it leads to very high spending.

US committees can also form strong bonds with pressure groups that reflect their area of interest and also the federal departments that they monitor. This three-way symbiotic relationship is known as an 'iron triangle'. President Nixon is said to have felt the power of these ties when he attempted to move the education of veterans from the control of the Veterans' Agency to the Department of Education. The agency resisted the move, the American Legion and other veterans' interest groups opposed the move, and the standing congressional Veterans' Affairs Committee condemned the decision and would not support it. President Nixon backed down.

US congressional committees also have a lot of investigative powers, such as over the Iran–Contra affair and the Watergate scandal. It was probably the investigative role of congressional committees that brought down President Nixon for his role in the Watergate affair.

However, the power of these organisations can be defended. Surely it is only right that members of Congress possess an expertise over certain areas of policy (indeed organisations such as the CBO, the Congressional Budget Office, have been set up to encourage this expertise within the legislature) so that Congress can more effectively check and balance the power of the executive branch. It is better that Congressmen and Senators who have a broad knowledge of all areas of policy, but are specialists in none, develop this expertise during their time in Congress.

Also, with the weak party system in Congress, it may be argued that it is necessary that Congressmen and Senators use their legislative and oversight power on committees and form 'voting blocks' by which they can most effectively exercise their own power and democratic mandate from the people who elected them. Furthermore, a symbiotic working relationship between a federal department, congressional committee and relevant interest groups can be seen as a way to take all views into account and create acceptable, well-thought-out policy. With

the federal government extending into people's lives as never before, it may be seen as desirable to have powerful organisations keeping a check on its every move. In the UK, standing and select committees are relatively weak, and the reputation of politicians is made on the floor of the House of Commons not in committees, unlike in the USA. Parliamentary committees are dominated to some degree by the executive, as their membership is chosen by the executive and the majority party has a major influence on how they work. The difference between the two countries can be seen in the reaction to intelligence failures, which were implicated in the decision to go to war in Iraq. The Foreign Relations standing committee in the US Congress used its full power and publicity to condemn major figures in the administration (which, in part, led to Karl Rove's resignation). The Foreign Affairs select committee in the UK had very little impact or media coverage. This means that in the USA the executive branch operates in conditions where it knows that its moves will be checked and its legislation will not pass unless thoroughly scrutinised by committees of Congress. Although much of the president's agenda may be blocked here, at least there is no 'executive dominance' as found in the Westminster Parliament.

📝 Although this answer lacks any great detail of the workings of congressional committees in legislative activity or oversight, it is still a highly effective and focused response to the question. It demonstrates excellent analytical skills and depth of understanding of congressional committees (AO2), which more than compensates for the lack of description of the committees at work. Counter-views are also very effectively covered as the candidate defends the power of the congressional committees in a highly evaluative way. Very impressive examples are deployed and comparisons are effectively made with some of the weaknesses of UK committees. In addition, the use of impressive political vocabulary and coverage of iron triangles make this answer worth a very high A grade.

■ ■ ■

C-grade answer

Standing committees in the Congress are more powerful and perform much more important roles than their UK counterparts. In the USA, standing committee stage comes after the first reading of the bill and before the second reading. In that stage, the standing committee has the power to decide whether or not the bill goes on to the second reading. Due to the large amount of bills coming before Congress, that is a very important function. (In the UK, standing committee would come after the second reading, where the main principles of the bill would have already been discussed. So committees don't have much power to influence the construction of a bill like in the USA.)

In the US system the committee stage of the bill is the most important part, as it consists of the policy specialists who consider the bill first and make all necessary amendments to it. They have the power to influence the substance of the bill by going through each point. Both UK and US standing committees would involve interest groups in the discussions on the bill.

US committees, as Bennett would argue, are more high-profile bodies, and are independent from the executive. This means that a president wouldn't be able to directly influence the outcome of the committee, unlike in the UK where committee members are influenced by the executive.

The US standing committees are said to be the main bodies inside Congress which actually legislate. Their power is enormous. They are the bodies which have close links with pressure groups and, therefore, this gives them extra power and prestige. Also, US standing committees have the very important role of scrutinising the executive, in addition to their legislative power. They can summon any executive member and have investigations into the executive's actions. As members of US committees are independent from the executive, it creates the environment for objective accountability. US committees are also highly financed. This is explained by the importance of their work and the scale of it, as most of the work is done there.

However, US committees are not totally powerful. Whatever they come up with in a bill has to be discussed by Congress. Even if it is approved it still has to go through final stages where two versions of the bill are compared by both chambers. The president would ultimately have the power to decide whether this bill becomes law or not (even though he can be overridden).

Standing committees in the Senate also have the power to approve the appointments made by the president, which further shows their power and influence in the US system.

🖉 This essay does not start well. Confusion over 'standing committee stages' inhibits the development of a coherent response to the actual question. An introductory paragraph discussing why the congressional committees are so powerful in the USA would provide more focus and would serve as a starting point of an answer demanding critical evaluation. This is introduced later into the answer, but it is done almost as an afterthought.

However, the candidate does demonstrate some knowledge and understanding of congressional committees and their role in legislation and oversight (AO1), although some of the debate is rather vague and lacks supporting evidence or detail, for example knowledge of the Conference Committee is only implied and there is no explanation of why links with pressure groups 'give them extra power'. There is a brief reference to the parliamentary committees in the UK, which is creditable but not especially informative. Other references to congressional committees, their resources, the president's ability to veto legislation and the Senate committees with confirmation power over presidential appointments are implied and gain some credit, but they are never fully developed with supporting evidence. The answer is therefore worth a high C grade but, with further development and examples, it could achieve a solid B.

The executive branch of government

(a) What factors does a president consider when choosing his cabinet? (10 marks)

e You need to recognise that cabinet construction is one of the first and most important tasks of an incoming president. Without a shadow cabinet to draw upon, the president has many factors to take into account when constructing a cabinet that will be acceptable to Congress, his party and the country. The more factors you can discuss to demonstrate your knowledge of this process, along with supporting evidence from recent presidencies, the higher your likely mark.

■ ■ ■

A-grade answer

The cabinet in the USA is by no means as important or powerful as its UK equivalent. The cabinet in the USA is an advisory body, not a decision-taking one, and this will certainly affect the president's choices. The president must bear in mind the need for Senate confirmation of his nominees so he cannot make too controversial a choice as they may be rejected, as George Bush's choice for defense secretary, John Tower, was in 1989.

When creating the cabinet, a US president looks for specialist knowledge and competence in the field of the federal department each person will represent. For example, George W. Bush's education adviser was head of the Texas state education board for many years. As a result he is only in the cabinet for education, holding no other post and not moving positions. (In the UK, cabinet ministers are selected for their political capabilities rather than expertise, as they are frequently reshuffled.) Presidents must concentrate on how they will get good policy advice, while prime ministers are more concerned with political characteristics and party support. In the USA, cabinet members are not rivals to the president and have no power base of their own.

Another factor taken into account by the president is the demographic make-up of the country and he may want to give broader appeal to his administration by making it more diverse and representative. This is not always the case, however, as Nixon's cabinet was said to be 'a dozen grey-haired men called George'. Clinton, on the other hand, wanted the cabinet to 'look like America' in terms of racial and gender factors. This can, however, be difficult due to the limited sources of cabinet members, who are often outgoing Congressmen or previous holders of influential positions. As a result of the fact that they must be experts in their field, it is difficult for presidents to create a culturally diverse cabinet, even if they wanted to.

As the US cabinet is only advisory to the president, it is less important for the president to fill it with political allies. It is usually said that presidents have a free hand when choosing, but G. W. Bush would have found it difficult not to appoint

Rumsfeld as defense secretary as he had been very influential in his father's administration. This is sometimes called 'cronyism'. However, all cabinet members must share the president's political objectives. Almost all cabinet members leave their posts when the president leaves office.

🖉 This is a fully focused answer, covering at least four factors influencing presidential choice, with examples and evidence given of four different presidents and their cabinet choices. There is a strong understanding of the US cabinet itself that comes through clearly in the answer, which is very well constructed and expressed. This answer scores high AO3 marks, as well as AO1 and AO2 marks, and would achieve a very comfortable A grade.

■ ■ ■

C-grade answer

There are several factors that must be taken into account by the president, as head of government, when he is creating his cabinet. The most prominent is the specific balance achieved within the cabinet. For example, the regional and political balance must be levelled to a degree that would satisfy both parties, due to the need for support from both parties to push through legislation and to confirm the appointments made. For example, Bill Clinton, a moderate Democrat, chose to sustain this balance by appointing Al Gore as his vice-president, another moderate.

Other factors taken into consideration include appointing a figure as a reward for support given in the past, for example in the election campaign, and, due to the vast recruitment pool available in the US, the president looks for specialist status and some kind of expertise in a certain policy field connected to the cabinet post itself.

🖉 The inclusion of one or two relevant points, covering cabinet balance and policy expertise, allow this answer just to scrape into the bottom of a C grade. Neither of these points, however, is fully developed with examples. The only example given is incorrect, that of Al Gore being selected as vice-president. The selection of a vice-president is done *before* the election, not as a cabinet post. Low C grade.

■ ■ ■

(b) Discuss the view that the president is effectively unconstrained in the exercise of executive power. (30 marks)

🖉 This question is asking not simply for knowledge of the powers of the president but whether the president is so powerful that he can, in effect, do what he likes. Your answer, therefore, should focus on possible constraints on the exercise of presidential power from numerous constitutional checks and balances, especially from Congress but also from other institutions and factors. You should recognise that presidents, no matter what the powers of the office, can be very weak or very

strong at different times. This will depend on variables such as personalities, circumstances and events, or domestic or foreign policy issues that, to achieve good marks, you would be expected to refer to in your answer. The imperial/imperilled debate and Neustadt's views on presidential power would be relevant here. You will need to include examples from different presidencies as evidence of constraints or lack of them.

■ ■ ■

A-grade answer

The US president is president within a presidential system of government but operating under the constraints of a codified constitution, which can significantly limit the exercise of his power, although not in all circumstances and at all times.

The president's position is as the figurehead of the country and the head of state because there is a sense of nationhood which he represents, giving him significant authority, although he is constrained by the separation of powers and the system of checks and balances laid down in the Constitution (unlike the UK prime minister, who is only the head of government with no separation of powers or legal entrenchment of checks and balances).

The president has many 'formal' powers from the Constitution and is the 'chief executive' with all executive power vested in him.

The president as chief executive has the power to make appointments into government, including his cabinet, for example. However, his appointments are subject to Senate confirmation as Senators have 'advice and consent powers' over his executive appointments, unlike the UK prime minister, whose appointments are not checked by the legislature.

The president is also known as 'chief legislator'. All bills must be presented to him and he can use his presidential veto or his 'pocket veto' (when near the end of a congressional session) but Congress can override his veto. The president makes a 'State of the Union Address' to propose legislation and the budget. However, Congress is under no obligation to accept his proposals. If two different parties control the executive and Congress this undermines the president's power in legislating (unlike the PM who, because of the fusion of power in the UK system, has control of Parliament through his majority and the whipping system).

The US president does have significant powers as chief diplomat. He can appoint ambassadors and make treaties but these require Senate ratification, which can be refused, as with the Versailles treaty in 1919.

The president, due to his frustration in domestic legislation, often concentrates more on foreign affairs where he has more authority and leeway to act, because Congress is much less willing to 'check' the president in this area and because there is a strong sense of nationhood and patriotism. However, presidents may also be frustrated in foreign affairs, and this has led to some presidents using illegal means to pursue foreign policy, for example Reagan and Irangate and Nixon's illegal bombing of Cambodia to pursue Vietnam policy. Nevertheless, the president's power in foreign policy is significant and may not be so constrained. As commander-in-chief the president can command the US forces of the army and navy. However, again his power can be 'effectively constrained' because only Congress can declare war and fund war. However, US forces fought for over 10 years in Vietnam without Congress declaring war.

The president has judicial power also. He can appoint federal judges, but his appointment powers are constrained by the need for Senate confirmation. For example, two of Nixon's appointees were rejected and Reagan's nomination of Bork was also rejected for being too right wing. Nevertheless, the president has significant power to alter the composition of the Supreme Court, for example in the Reagan/Bush years conservative judges were put on the Supreme Court and in the Clinton years the Supreme Court had new liberal judges on it.

So the power of the president varies. He certainly has power but he cannot always exercise it and it is subject to numerous constraints and effectively checked and balanced, particularly by Congress. The president has significant authority on a world scale because the USA is considered a superpower and he has a greater role in global politics where he has more freedom of action to operate.

🖉 Although looking at times almost like a list of presidential powers, this answer does present a large amount of knowledge, shows understanding of the presidential role and is illustrated throughout with relevant evidence and examples of some presidents. It would gain high marks for AO1 but less for AO2. The answer is communicated well, with knowledge and analysis used from AS studies, and with good use of political vocabulary, so would gain high AO3 marks. It begins well and ends with a convincing conclusion pertinent to the question. Overall, this answer would achieve a grade A.

■ ■ ■

C-grade answer

Many political scientists have made a case showing the increasing power of the US executive, using phrases such as 'Emperor President', and this view can be supported by much evidence.

The Constitution gives the president all executive power. He is commander-in-chief of the armed forces and head of state, and although Congress is supposed to decide upon war, increasingly, for example in Iraq in 2003 and several times under Clinton before, the president has found ways to usurp this power.

Since the 1930s, the president's power has also been increased by the growth of EXOP, which began under Roosevelt and from which more powerful presidents, e.g. Nixon, have chosen to run policy. In the USA, cabinet meetings occur infrequently. Aided by the fact that he is the only directly elected figure at the meeting,

the president is head of the discussions, unlike in the UK where the prime minister is 'first among equals' in cabinet and makes joint decisions with his cabinet colleagues.

In the USA, the president does not require support from his own party to retain power — for example, Clinton from 1994 onwards had a minority in both houses of Congress but continued as president, even though Congress voted against many of his proposals — whereas in the UK a prime minister would not be able to carry on without party support, as Callaghan and Thatcher found to their cost. However, it is worth considering that in 1974 Nixon resigned before impeachment after losing party support. The president does, however, have limited means of keeping his party in check (principally due to the separation of powers) when rarely he might need it, as the people decide in primaries who they wish to select, and the congressional whip system is weaker, the political spectrum wider.

Also, due to the increased media focus and influence, it is possible the position of the president has gained in stature. He is seen as the face of his party in increased coverage and consequently the perception of his power at least may have increased.

However, the president is not always unopposed, as has been alluded to before. The separation of powers and checks made by other bodies, for example impeachment in the Congress and Congress's ability to override the presidential veto (used twice on Clinton's 36 vetoes) and the judiciary's power to declare any actions of the executive unconstitutional. Power also depends on the president himself and the economic or military situations. For example, Roosevelt's presidency was powerful due to the depression of the 1930s, and Nixon's due to his personality.

In conclusion, the power of the president is large and has increased in the last 100 years. However, to say that he is entirely unrestrained would not be an accurate picture as numerous checks and balances along with the personalities of leaders do act to vary and limit their power, which fluctuates according to the situation of the government and the country in general.

This answer, although very knowledgeable in parts (so worth some high AO1 marks), is not completely focused on the actual question. The analytical arguments, such as those relating to EXOP or the cabinet, are rather vague and not fully developed or linked to the question (thus lowering possible AO2 marks). Also, although the candidate makes several points from AS studies of the UK prime minister, which is creditable, these are not always effectively made or closely related to the question. The same can be said of the examples used by the candidate. How and why has the president 'found ways to usurp' the war powers, for example? Why would power 'depend on the president himself'? To raise the mark above a C grade, you would need to focus clearly on the numerous constitutional constraints on the exercise of presidential power and provide some analysis of how different presidents attempt to circumvent these in order to carry out their presidential agendas.

The judicial branch of government: the Supreme Court

(a) Explain what is meant by judicial independence.   (10 marks)

This question is looking for knowledge and contextual understanding of the key concept of judicial independence, which you should be careful not to confuse with judicial impartiality or neutrality. A good answer should focus on the importance of keeping the judiciary independent from the other branches of government, the executive and the legislature, without any influence or control from them over judicial decisions, especially when many of these decisions have political effects in the USA because of judicial review. It is essential that you show knowledge of how independence is achieved, such as security of tenure or protection of salaries, if you are to gain high marks.

■ ■ ■

A-grade answer

An independent judiciary is simply a judiciary that can act of its own accord without any politicisation or indeed without any influence from the other branches of government. In the USA, the Constitution clearly gives the judiciary independence through the separation of powers, a factor in the legitimacy of judicial review over acts of Congress and the president. As such, with checks and balances on both other branches, the Supreme Court maintains an independent position in which it is able to declare both acts of Congress and the executive branch as unconstitutional without influence or control from either. Importantly, judicial independence is far removed from judicial impartiality, referring to the resistance of politicisation, because judges hold their positions until incapacitated and maintain a fixed salary, thus removing the possibility of influence because of their stance taken over ideological issues. The independence of the Supreme Court was, however, threatened during the 1930s when President Roosevelt tried to pack the court with favourable candidates in order to manipulate a decision.

Although a little convoluted in expression at times, this answer effectively pins down the meaning of the term and clearly distinguishes it from judicial neutrality. The reference to concepts such as the separation of powers and judicial review puts the answer firmly in the higher level for marks on AO2 and AO3. Evidence of how judicial independence is maintained means high AO1 marks and the final sentence demonstrates, through an example, the way independence could be threatened. This is an excellent response worthy of a high grade A.

■ ■ ■

question

C-grade answer

In a democracy it is extremely important for the judiciary to remain both independent and neutral. The judiciary should be independent of other branches of government so it can make decisions without any outside interference.

Judicial independence is clearly demonstrated in the USA where judges have the right to independence through the Constitution. However, as the president has the power to nominate senior judges (albeit with the advice and consent of the Senate) this can lead to presidents nominating judges with similar political philosophies to their own.

Senior judges cannot be removed from office except for misconduct and judges are free from restraints such as the need to win re-election, unlike politicians, therefore their independence is maintained.

The first paragraph suggests that the concept of judicial independence is understood but the second paragraph does not 'clearly demonstrate' why there is judicial independence 'through the Constitution' and the answer strays too far into neutrality rather than independence. However, the final paragraph has enough content to lift the answer into a C grade. Clearer definitions, reference to concepts such as the separation of powers and some supporting examples or evidence would be necessary to lift the mark further.

■ ■ ■

(b) 'Politicians sitting on a bench'. How accurate is this description of the US Supreme Court? (30 marks)

The question is referring to the debate surrounding the politicisation of the judicial branch of government and the extent of its 'political' as opposed to its 'judicial' role. Your answer will need to include analysis relating to the appointment process of justices, with examples of controversial political appointments, and the judicial philosophies of activism and restraint and the 'loose' and 'strict' constructionism of constitutional interpretation, with examples from landmark cases, or different courts, to show evidence (or not) of any politicisation of the Supreme Court.

■ ■ ■

A-grade answer

The description is suggesting that members of the Supreme Court are 'politicians' rather than justices and this is open to debate.

In the USA, the Supreme Court was set up by the Constitution and the justices are senior members of the judiciary, usually with vast legal experience. It is the appointment process of these justices, and the role that they play, which may lead to them being described as 'politicians'. In the USA the process has been described as highly politicised, with the president nominating a nominee and the Senate confirming the nomination. One nominee, Samuel Alito, is currently being questioned and his experience tested by the Judiciary Committee in the Senate with lots of media attention given to it, demonstrating the importance of the Supreme Court and the belief that Bush nominated Alito to please the conservative right of his supporters.

Presidents generally nominate people who are likely to reflect their ideological views on the court. However, Eisenhower nominated Chief Justice Earl Warren as a conservative but the Warren Court's decisions turned out to be the most liberal in the court's history.

Apart from looking at the appointment process, which seems to be more overtly political in the USA than in the UK, although that could be due to the physical separation of the Supreme Court from the other branches, one can also look at the roles, functions and powers of the judiciary to see whether their actions suggest that they are really 'politicians' and not judges.

The Supreme Court's jurisdiction is laid out in Article 3 of the Constitution. However, after the 1803 *Marbury* v *Madison* and 1819 *McCulloch* v *Maryland* cases, precedents were set concerning judicial review. In accordance with these two cases the Supreme Court could rule as to whether state legislatures or the federal government were acting unconstitutionally. This precedent has remained out of respect for the sovereignty of the Constitution and places the Supreme Court at the heart of decision making, and the court has struck down over 700 state laws and 80 federal laws as unconstitutional, thus overruling the elected bodies. Other rulings show that the Supreme Court is a body which can have much 'political' influence. The case of *Roe* v *Wade* in 1973 and subsequent cases concerned abortion and the *Brown* v *Board of Education of Topeka* case led to the end of segregation — decisions that could be deemed to be 'political'. On the other hand, it could be argued that these decisions were based on the interpretation of the words of the Constitution. However, the tendency for most justices to rule according to the ideology they believe in, and the change that comes about from the court reinterpreting decisions, suggest these rulings are indeed political, and they certainly have political consequences.

Similarly, the Supreme Court ensures that civil rights and liberties are fully protected with a contextual interpretation of the Constitution (known as loose construction of the words of the Constitution in the modern context), such as the cases seen above. The court even decided the outcome of the 2000 election in the *Bush* v *Gore* case when it ruled that the recount of ballots in Florida was unconstitutional, which many saw as a 'political' decision by justices appointed by past Republican presidents. However, the court has to wait for cases to come before it and not all cases will be heard.

The Supreme Court has gone through periods of both judicial activism, such as the Warren Court where it made more 'liberal' rulings, but also periods of judicial

restraint when it refuses to hear cases and is regarded as a more conservative court. It is regarded as being more 'political' with the former rather than the latter.

American people see the justices on the court as their judicial and constitutional representatives acting as a check on the other branches of government and protecting their rights and liberties. In the UK, the Law Lords' verdicts using judicial review also have political consequences, such as the recent ban on evidence obtained from torture, but this was not perceived as being anti-Labour. In contrast, the decisions the Supreme Court reaches on issues like abortion seem to arise more from the justices' political views rather than their reading of the Constitution itself, hence 'politicians sitting on a bench'.

This answer is very focused on the question and keeps the focus throughout the essay. It covers a lot of ground in relation to the appointment process, the importance of judicial review, through to discussion of judicial philosophy and different kinds of courts, such as liberal or conservative, activist or restrained. The political language and vocabulary used is impressive and the essay shows clear understanding of the role of the Supreme Court. This means high marks for all three assessment objectives. Evidence and examples are also given from cases decided by the court. Some reference is made to the UK Law Lords, demonstrating progression from AS. This is a well-argued A-grade response.

■ ■ ■

C-grade answer

In the USA it is generally accepted that Supreme Court justices are somewhat political especially when compared to the Law Lords in the UK. Supreme Court justices are appointed by the president but only if the Senate approves their appointment. The Senate approval of the judges is a way of making sure that the Supreme Court does not become too biased towards one political viewpoint. Currently there is a debate in the USA as to who will replace Sandra Day O'Connor. The president [G. W. Bush] hopes that his choice, Sam Alito, will be approved. However, this would mean the Supreme Court would be biased towards the conservatives. Alito is considered a hard-line conservative but Sandra Day O'Connor was considered a 'swing vote'. This is an example of the legislative wing acting as a barrier to the Supreme Court becoming too politically biased. In the UK Law Lords are appointed by the prime minister, but appointments are not made because of their political views but because of their experience and reputation.

US Supreme Court justices are appointed for life. This means that a president rarely gets to choose more than one justice, if any at all. This is another way in which the court is stopped from becoming politically biased; because the justices remain the same from government to government it generally means that when the time comes to appoint a new judge the same president isn't in power and often it is a different party to the last time, meaning opinions in the executive and legislative wings will have changed and the Supreme Court will not be manipulated towards either a strong conservative or liberal majority.

There are examples of judges in the USA effectively making law and in some cases changing the Constitution. In these cases, for example *Roe* v *Wade*, the political bias of the court is extremely important. In *Roe* v *Wade* the right to abortion was challenged: Mrs Roe, who resided in Texas, wanted the right to have an abortion, which was illegal at that time. The case went to the Supreme Court and it was up to the court to decide whether or not to change the law on abortion. The outcome was that the liberal judges won and the law was changed to allow abortion in all the states; however, the states did not have to, and still do not have to, fund abortion clinics. This is a clear example of political bias in the Supreme Court having an impact on citizens and does somewhat support the claim that the Supreme Court justices are 'politicians sitting on a bench'.

The United States judiciary are more politicised than the Law Lords in the UK. When a president has to appoint a justice he will try as hard as possible to get a judge in who will tip the balance of the Supreme Court towards their own and their party's views. In the UK judges are appointed for different reasons and political opinion rarely comes into it. The Supreme Court judges are 'politicians sitting on a bench' to a substantial degree.

✓ This essay, although in the main quite knowledgeable and focused, does not completely get to grips with the question and lacks clarity and coherence of argument. The discussion of the appointment process could be improved by some examples of appointments made (or rejected, such as Bork in 1987) for political reasons. The two appointments made by Bush in 2005–6 would be good examples to discuss. Some arguments need much more developed explanation, e.g. why would Alito's approval mean the court would be 'biased towards the conservatives'? What is a 'swing vote' on the court? Why are justices 'effectively making law' by their decisions? The selection of the Roe case is a good choice but the candidate does not make the most of it. In fact the third paragraph becomes unclear narrative, so the impact of the *Roe* v *Wade* decision in 1973 on the debate about politicisation is effectively lost. However, there is just enough analysis and focus, with some backing evidence on the political role of justices in the USA, for the answer to achieve a low grade C.